# A HIGHER
# STANDARD OF
# LEADERSHIP

# A HIGHER STANDARD OF LEADERSHIP

Lessons from
the Life of
Gandhi

## KESHAVAN NAIR

Berrett-Koehler Publishers
San Francisco

**Berrett-Koehler Publishers, Inc.**
450 Sansome Street, Suite 1200
San Francisco, CA 94111-3320
Tel: (415) 288-0260  Fax: (415) 362-2512

ORDERING INFORMATION
**Individual sales**
Special discounts are available on quantity purchases by corporations, associations, and others. For details, contact the "Special Sales Department" at the Berrett-Koehler address above.

**Orders for college textbook/course adoption use**
Please contact Berrett-Koehler Publishers at the address above.

**Orders by U.S. trade bookstores and wholesalers**
Please contact: Publishers Group West
4065 Hollis Street, Box 8843, Emeryville, CA 94662
Tel: (510) 658-3453; 1-800-788-3123  Fax: (510) 658-1834

**Printed in the United States of America**
Printed on acid-free and recycled paper that is composed of 85% recovered fiber, including 15% post-consumer waste.

**Library of Congress Cataloging-in-Publication Data**
Nair, Keshavan, 1932–
     A Higher Standard of Leadership / Keshavan Nair. — 1st ed.
         p.    cm.
     Includes bibliographical references and index.
     ISBN 1-881052-58-3 (hardcover: alk paper)
     ISBN 1-57675-011-6 (paperback: alk paper)
     1. Leadership — Moral and ethical aspects. 2. Gandhi, Mahatma, 1869–1948.
I. Title
HM141.N33  1994              94-26927
303.3'4 — dc20                        CIP
First Hardcover Printing: October 1994
First Paperback Printing: January 1997
             03  04  05  06    10 9 8 7
This paperback edition contains the complete text of the original hardcover edition.

Editing: **Elaine de Man**
Cover design: **Cassandra Chu**
Book design and production: **Candace Pappas**
Gandhi's writings are quoted with permission of the Navajivan Trust, Ahmedabad India. Photos on pages 10 and 56 are by Margaret Bourke-White, *Life Magazine* © Time Warner, photo on page 94 is by Wallace Kirkland, *Life Magazine* © Time Warner.

To

Parvathi Bai Nair

Leila Ramakumar

Robba Benjamin

*Leaders with Higher Standards*

# CONTENTS

# PREFACE

Like most Indians of my generation, I can tell you where I was and what I was doing when Gandhi was assassinated on the evening of January 30, 1948. I had gone skating at a rink located in a park about a ten-minute walk from our house in Patiala, a city in the Punjab. It was dark, I was returning home, and two people on bicycles passed me. One of them said to the other, "The old man is dead." At that moment I did not know whom they were talking about. When I reached home five minutes later, the radio was on and everybody was in tears. As I walked through the door somebody said, "Gandhiji has been killed."

I was fifteen when Gandhi was assassinated. He was a revered figure in our home, but he held no special appeal for me. His emphasis on renunciation, and the emphasis that was placed on his saintliness, were outside the frame of reference of a boy who had been sent to an English-style public school and whose prime interests were cricket, movies, and schoolwork. Of all the national leaders it had always been easiest for me to identify with Jawaharlal Nehru—educated at Harrow and Cambridge, urbane and sophisticated—who later became India's first prime minister.

And so it remained until I was nineteen, when I fell ill and was confined to bed for two years. There was much time for reading. When I read Nehru's autobiography, I learned of his admiration for Gandhi's commitment to his ideals and of Gandhi's strength and courage. "And in spite of his unimpressive features," wrote Nehru, "his loin-cloth and bare body, there was a royalty and a kingliness in him which compelled a willing obeisance from others."[1]

In the hurry of my youth, my evaluation of Gandhi had been, to say the least, superficial. I embarked on a reading and study program and came to realize that Gandhi was not a saint. Making him into one was to do him a disservice: it made it too easy to categorize his life and ideas as impractical—which is exactly what I had done. I began to understand the heroic nature of the man in his willingness to address fundamental questions and then to try with all his being to live by the answers he found. I developed an appreciation of his personal courage, his faith in human nature, and his spirit of service. I realized there was a majesty to Gandhi that came from his inner strength. I became convinced that, among those leaders who had been engaged in social and political activities of any significant scale, Gandhi stood alone in representing the best in the human spirit. He was a man of action who devoted his life to service within the context of politics and social reform, always striving—though not always succeeding—to live up to his ideals of truth and nonviolence.

With the enthusiasm of a convert, I decided to do what I could to bring some symbolic aspects of Gandhi's teachings into my life. I began spinning and gave up several minor conveniences and silks and gabardines for handwoven handspun cloth, practices I continued until I left for the United States in 1959.

For the past thirty-five years, I have been busy obtaining advanced degrees, progressing in my profession, and acquiring those material things that make life comfortable and enjoyable. My management and consulting activities have included assignments with entrepreneurial companies, small established companies, and Fortune 100 companies. I have functioned as the principal investigator and project manager on large multidisciplinary teams and as a senior operating executive and director of a large professional service firm. I have provided counsel to senior executives on leadership issues related to strategy and implementation and have experienced and observed leadership challenges and activities in a wide variety of contexts.

In all my professional activities, the example of Gandhi's leadership was always in the background. As 1994 is the 125th anniversary of Gandhi's birth, it is an appropriate time to place certain aspects of his leadership within the context of current leadership concepts and tasks, particularly since there seems to be a widely held view that our leaders, especially those in business and politics, have lost their idealism and sense of moral purpose.

This is not a book on Gandhi. What I have attempted to do is to develop a leadership framework within which lessons drawn from Gandhi's life can be used to bring the moral and spiritual dimension to leadership and guide us to a higher standard.

Selecting examples from Gandhi's life to illustrate leadership concepts was a challenge—there were so many from which to choose. I have chosen those that I felt could be easily explained to today's reader. There are other more powerful examples, but they would require lengthy explanations of Indian conditions and ways of life, making the book difficult to read without adding significantly to the message.

The qualities that Gandhi exemplified, such as personal responsibility, truth, love, respect for the individual, and courage, have applications throughout our work and social lives. This book espouses a concept of leadership heroic in its commitment to moral principles and service rather than one driven by the acquisition of power and mastering the forces of violence. It is this kind of heroic leadership that we must place before the youth in this country— leadership that can harness the ideals in all of us, appeal to what is best in us, and move us to a better quality of life.

We all have leadership roles, from presidents and CEOs to parents, elders, and teachers who have the opportunity and obligation to influence the youth of the world. Those of us not in power have a responsibility to raise our standards so our leaders will have to follow.

Because I believe it is up to each of us to move toward a higher standard of leadership, the emphasis in this book is on individual responsibility. It is at the individual level that we must commit to principled actions and service. I do not believe it is necessary to follow or focus on Gandhi's ascetic lifestyle to benefit from his example. I appreciate the material world. However, because of my appreciation of Gandhi, I find that my standards of conduct in my professional and social life are higher. I hope my dealings with others reflect this. Maybe that is the legacy of any individual, great or ordinary: to have a positive influence on the lives of others.

*San Francisco, California*                                        *—Keshavan Nair*
*August 1994*

# ACKNOWLEDGMENTS

Kathryn Hall has encouraged this project from its inception and was instrumental in bringing the book to the attention of the publisher, Steven Piersanti. Steven and the staff at Berrett-Koehler Publishers have been generous in their support during the writing and publication of this book. Ellen Carr typed many drafts of the manuscript, and her caring attitude toward her work has always served as an example for me. I was extremely fortunate to have Elaine de Man as my editor; her demands for clarity and economy in words have improved the book immeasurably. Any deficiencies in these areas are mine alone. Finally, everything I do is better because I know Robba Benjamin. To all these individuals I wish to express my thanks.

# Introduction:
# The Challenge
# of a Higher Standard

Today, many people believe that it is not possible to be successful in the world of business and politics and still to maintain one's integrity—integrity not defined by absence of financial corruption, but by adherence to moral principles in all activities. Many have also come to believe that a major purpose of leadership is to acquire power and privilege. And many believe that practical political and business decisions would be less effective if serious consideration were given to moral issues.

The standard of leadership depends not only on the qualities and beliefs of our leaders but also on the expectations we have of them. As long we believe that our leaders lack integrity, our expectations are likely to

*The standard of leadership depends not only on the qualities and beliefs of our leaders but also on the expectations we have of them.*

be mirrored in their conduct. Therefore, it is up to each of us to improve our own standard of leadership and thus raise our expectations of those who would lead us.

In putting forward a path to a higher standard of leadership, there is no greater exemplar than Mohandas Karamchand Gandhi. Gandhi spent more than fifty years in public life and is best known for leading hundreds of millions of people against one of the greatest empires in the history of the world. In contrast to the other political leaders and military commanders of his time—men such as Hitler, Mussolini, Stalin, Churchill, Roosevelt, de Gaulle, Eisenhower, Montgomery, Patton, and MacArthur—Gandhi wore no resplendent uniform, commanded no armies, and held no government position. Instead he preached and—more importantly—lived the gospel of truth and nonviolence and demonstrated through his life of service the oneness of all humanity. He reminded the world that the human spirit is indomitable and that courage and love are more powerful than force. The world acknowledged his special place when the United Nations flew its flag at half-mast when he was assassinated. He is the only individual with no connection to any government or international organization for whom this has been done.

Gandhi had many of the qualities we associate with

> *In putting forward a path to a higher standard of leadership, there is no greater exemplar than Mohandas Karamchand Gandhi.*

successful leaders. In addition to courage and determination, he could sustain a high energy level for
extended periods, he was decisive, he had great interpersonal skills, he was thoughtful but action oriented, and
he paid great attention to the details of implementation.

Gandhi's life was not governed by policies; it was
governed by principles and values. The best political
leaders have their country as the source of their passion.
Business leaders have as their passion the organization,
whether it is through customers, products, or technology.
Gandhi's life was driven by his religion: truth and nonviolence and a life of service to others. When a journalist
asked Gandhi for a message for the United States,
especially for African Americans, Gandhi responded,
"My life is its own message."[2]

Those who have seen the film *Gandhi* know of his
work in the political arena—the struggle for freedom
from discrimination for Indians in South Africa and,
later, the movement for independence from British rule
in India. But the full scope of Gandhi's activities goes
beyond what any leader in public life has ever
attempted. (A list of suggested readings is given in the
back of this book for those who wish to develop a
greater understanding of the range of his thoughts and
actions.)

*Gandhi's life
was not governed
by policies;
it was governed
by principles
and values.*

*Gandhi believed that all religions were manifestations of the Truth and that people of different faiths should and could live in peace and harmony.*

In the area of social reform, Gandhi's major focus was the abolition of untouchability, an integral component of Hinduism, the predominant religion in India. Over the centuries, Hinduism had developed a hierarchical and hereditary caste system. Many Hindus believed—and some still believe—that if an individual of a lower caste touched them, they would become "unclean." Individuals in the lowest group in this system were called "untouchables."

Untouchables numbered in the tens of millions— about one-fifth the population of India. They were forced to live in separate areas and were not allowed to use the same public facilities, including the temples, that the rest of the Hindus used. The most insidious component of this discrimination was that the untouchables believed that this terrible treatment was sanctioned by their own religion.

Gandhi spent a major part of his life trying to abolish untouchability. He coined the term *harijan* (child of God) to use instead of untouchable. He worked to give untouchables equal status under the umbrella of Hinduism and was resisted not only by conservative Hindus, but also by some of the untouchables, who wanted to separate themselves from Hinduism to achieve political parity and to accelerate reform.

In the arena of economic reform, Gandhi's prime focus was on improving the condition of the villagers, who constituted the majority of Indians and were very poor. He developed programs to bring education, sanitation, and public health to the villages. At the same time he wanted the villagers to help themselves by developing village industries. Gandhi concentrated on spinning and weaving. He argued that if those in the villages would spin and make yarn that could be woven into cloth at the village level, they would have a source of income to support the family's part-time farm labor income. Gandhi also called on the rest of India to support the cause of the villagers by wearing only handwoven handspun cloth. To show solidarity with the villagers, Gandhi spun every day of his life and wore only hand-woven handspun cloth.

Gandhi believed in the equality of all forms of labor. He developed and participated in the labor union movement and never asked any of his followers to do work he would not do himself.

Gandhi believed that all religions were manifestations of the Truth and that people of different faiths should and could live in peace and harmony. He devoted a great part of his life to eliminating violence and promoting mutual respect and tolerance between Hindus

*The lessons from Gandhi's life challenge our beliefs about the standards of leadership — beliefs that many of us have come to accept as necessary for success.*

*Gandhi believed in a single standard of conduct in public and private life— a standard founded on integrity derived from the absolute values of truth and nonviolence.*

and Muslims. He wanted to maintain an undivided India in which Hindus and Muslims could live in peace after independence—thus avoiding the creation of Pakistan. In this he was not successful.

At a personal level Gandhi spent a great deal of his life in an ashram, best described as a spiritual community. Everyone who lived in the ashram had to live in voluntary poverty, reject untouchability, commit themselves to truth and nonviolence, and accept equal responsibility for the labor necessary to make the ashram self-sufficient. It was at the ashram that Gandhi had colleagues who shared his commitment to spiritual values and from whom he could draw support and renew himself.

The lessons from Gandhi's life challenge our beliefs about the standards of leadership—beliefs that many of us have come to accept as necessary for success. While most leaders identify with symbols of power to elevate themselves above the people they lead, Gandhi symbolized the people he was trying to serve. He tried to be like them with his loin cloth and his commitment to voluntary poverty. He symbolized service rather than power.

Gandhi believed in a single standard of conduct in public and private life—a standard founded on integrity derived from the absolute values of truth and nonviolence. He believed that individuals must have ideals and try to live up to them, and he demonstrated that an idealist could be practical and effective. His claim, however, was to integrity, not infallibility. He made his share of mistakes but was not afraid to acknowledge them. He did not strive for consistency except in his quest for the truth.

As all policies, strategies, and laws ultimately have an impact on people or the environment, Gandhi believed that moral principles had to be included in setting goals, selecting strategies, and making decisions. He worked for the betterment of all people so they could enjoy freedom from fear and exploitation.

Some of Gandhi's ideas may seem irrelevant today—applicable only to his time and place. But on the fundamental values of truth, nonviolence, and service, he had a message for the ages. He asked us to reject not only physical violence, but violence to the spirit. It becomes more self-evident every day, that if we do not embrace his ideal of nonviolence, societies all over the world will deteriorate to the point where life will be intolerable.

Today we talk about controlling physical violence with more violence and controlling spiritual violence

*On the fundamental values of truth, nonviolence, and service, he had a message for the ages. He asked us to reject not only physical violence, but violence to the spirit.*

*We need a new heroic ideal: the brave, truthful, nonviolent individual who is in the service of humanity, resists injustice and exploitation, and leads by appealing to our ideals and our spirit. Such a heroic ideal is embodied in Gandhi.*

with laws. Maybe it is necessary. But I believe that the only long-term solution is to put before us, especially the young, the ideal of nonviolence—not the nonviolence of the coward, but the nonviolence of the brave. We need a new heroic ideal: the brave, truthful, nonviolent individual who is in the service of humanity, resists injustice and exploitation, and leads by appealing to our ideals and our spirit. Such a heroic ideal is embodied in Gandhi.

Gandhi's life points the way to a higher standard of leadership in which integrity based on a single standard of conduct is central, a spirit of service is imperative, and decisions and actions are bound by moral principles.

Lessons from Gandhi's life challenge us as individuals to play our part in fostering and living up to a higher standard. If you are preparing for leadership, this book can assist you in establishing ideals, show you how to move toward them, and thus set you on the path. If you are already in a leadership position with power and privilege, this book will challenge you to look at your conduct and set yourself a higher standard.

# PART 1

# A Single
# Standard
# of Conduct

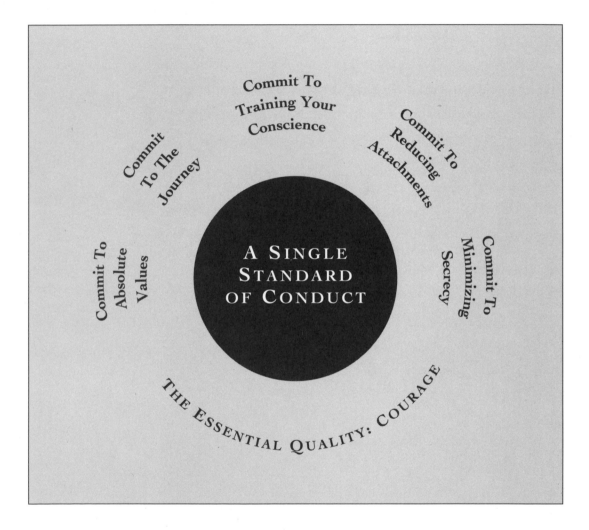

We have been led to believe that there is one standard for private morality and conduct and another for public morality and conduct. We have come to accept that a lower moral standard is necessary to get things done in the real world of politics and business. This is the gospel of expediency—the double standard of conduct. It is fueled by the idea of winning at all costs: that results are the only things that count.

The evidence that many subscribe to the double standard is everywhere. Politicians ask us to judge them on their legislative accomplishments, not on their personal conduct. Social activists who claim the high moral ground in their personal philosophy use violence to obtain results. Business executives do not want their conduct examined but ask us instead to focus exclusively on the bottom line. And many journalists who maintain a personal commitment to the truth succumb to the pressures of wanting to be first and, rather than wait for the whole story, publish half-truths.

When leadership sets the example, the double standard permeates the organization. In business, new employees who wish to succeed quickly understand how the game is played, and many forsake their ideals to achieve success. Most of us have been to meetings where we have watched someone take credit for work

*We have come to accept that a lower moral standard is necessary to get things done in the real world of politics and business. This is the gospel of expediency— the double standard of conduct.*

*The reality
is that we lose
respect for
our leaders
if we do not
approve of
their conduct—
public or private.
Leaders who
do not command
our respect reduce
the legitimacy
of their
leadership
and lose our trust.*

they have not done. We have observed individuals deliberately withhold data and resources to reduce their colleagues' chances for success. This acceptance of a lower standard is also prevalent outside the corporate and political arena—from the consultant or lawyer who adds a few extra hours when billing clients, to the garage mechanic who charges for work not done, to individuals who submit inflated insurance claims.

Being an adult—an elder or a parent—is in many ways being at the front line of leadership. Many years ago I was in a restaurant, sitting at a table next to a couple and their daughter who was in her early teens. When the credit card receipt came, the father wrote something on the back of it. The daughter picked it up, examined it, and said rather loudly, "But he wasn't with us at dinner." The parents looked at each other in silence. Here, the double standard of conduct was brought into focus at the most fundamental level: in a family, by a child. The parents, not thinking of the example they were setting, had demonstrated that it was appropriate to lie under some circumstances, and the child had been introduced to the double standard. Setting an example is central to the leadership role.

To defend the double standard, some people point to the facts that many individuals with questionable private morality perform outstanding public service and that many individuals whose conduct in public life is suspect are good family members and friends. This is true. But the reality is that we lose respect for our leaders if we do not approve of their conduct—public or private. Leaders who do not command our respect reduce the legitimacy of their leadership and lose our trust. Leaders who are not trusted find it difficult to challenge others to greatness. This not only makes leadership less effective, but leads to a general decline in the hopes of society. We feel helpless and get cynical because we cannot trust our leaders. There is a deterioration of our soul.

In the history of public leadership, there has never been an individual as committed to a single standard of conduct in private and public life as Gandhi. He believed and acted on the belief that leaders have the responsibility to set an example of conduct. Gandhi rejected compartmentalization. His political life was no different from his personal life, and both were based on his religion. "You must watch my life," he said, "how I live, eat, sit, talk, behave in general. The sum total of all those in me is my religion."[3]

To increase legitimacy and respect for leadership and for the system in which we live, we must acknowledge Gandhi's ideal of a single standard—a single

*To increase legitimacy and respect for leadership and for the system in which we live, we must acknowledge Gandhi's ideal of a single standard— a single standard of conduct in both public and private life.*

*When we
lose our ideals,
we lack depth
as individuals,
we stop thinking
and striving
to improve,
and most
importantly
we lose
our kinship
with others.*

standard of conduct in both public and private life. This is not a call for perfection; it is something to measure our actions against—something to strive for and to help us control our imperfections.

Debates about economic and business theories such as free markets, the role of government, profit maximization, and competitive strategies do not impact the character of leadership or society. But our adherence to the ideal of a single standard does. Ideals are food for the soul. When we lose our ideals, we lack depth as individuals, we stop thinking and striving to improve, and most importantly we lose our kinship with others. It is this loss of kinship that fuels the spiritual and physical violence around us. To create a harmonious society economic progress must be surrounded by a commitment to ideals. To paraphrase what was said two thousand years ago: "What will a nation gain through economic progress if it loses its soul?"

It is not enough to exhort people to live by a single standard; we have to make it practical. We need guidelines that individuals in all segments of our society—from potential leaders in our high schools and universities to parents and teachers, from leaders in our communities to national and international leaders—can understand and try to follow. We must lay before ourselves a process for striving toward a single standard. Each individual will see his or her own way within this process.

Striving toward an ideal requires commitment. This is no different than trying to achieve excellence in any field of endeavor—from sports to science, from music to mathematics. There are, however, two important differences. Striving for an ideal with respect to individual conduct is more difficult because it encompasses everything we do. On the other hand, each of us has the potential to achieve excellence—we can all think of ourselves as gifted.

After examining Gandhi's legacy, I have identified five basic commitments that lead to a higher standard of leadership:

- Develop a basis for the single standard: Commit to absolute values
- Acknowledge the ideal: Commit to the journey
- Develop the guide that will keep you on the journey: Commit to training your conscience
- Reduce forces that lead you astray: Commit to reducing attachments
- Be willing to stand scrutiny: Commit to minimizing secrecy

*Striving for an ideal with respect to individual conduct is difficult because it encompasses everything we do. On the other hand, each of us has the potential to achieve excellence— we can all think of ourselves as gifted.*

*Each of us
must make a
commitment
to live by a
single standard
of conduct —
for if we do,
our leaders
will have to follow.*

I believe what makes striving toward a single standard particularly difficult in a leadership context is that many of the practice sessions are done in public. To use an analogy, falls on the ice and wrong notes are seen and heard by everyone. Courage is the essential personal quality required to maintain the five basic commitments; as exemplified by Gandhi's life, this is courage of the spirit linked to an indomitable will. Each of us must make a commitment to live by a single standard of conduct — for if we do, our leaders will have to follow.

## 1

# Develop a
# Basis for the
# Single Standard

## Commit to Absolute Values

In every field of human endeavor, we search for universal principles that will bring order to chaos. In science we look for unifying theories and laws; in business we look for strategic concepts to guide decision making. To grow as human beings, to guide our conduct, we also look for universal principles: absolute values.

Absolute values can come from a religious perspective—an attempt to get the individual closer to what is divine—or directly from codes of conduct. While Gandhi's basis was undoubtedly religious, he embraced the fundamental directive basic to every religion and culture: to treat other human beings as ourselves. Absolute values are necessary in every field, whether you are a student or teacher, parent or child, manager

*To grow as human beings, to guide our conduct, we also look for universal principles: absolute values.*

*Leaders have the greatest responsibility. Without the compass of absolute values, what instrument do they have to guide others?*

or employee, politician or constituent. Leaders, however, have the greatest responsibility. Without the compass of absolute values, what instrument do they have to guide others?

Gandhi formulated two absolute values: truth and nonviolence. They were linked together, both ends in themselves and means to an end—faces of the same coin.

Gandhi's definition of truth was broad: "There should be Truth in thought, Truth in speech and Truth in action."4 When truth controls action, we move toward complete congruence between words and deeds. This is *living truthfully*—thinking and acting truthfully.

To Gandhi, God was truth. In this sense Gandhi gave a religious meaning to the expression, "You shall know the truth and the truth shall make you free." The level of your personal commitment in the search for truth will determine your commitment to truth in dealing with others. This is the basis of the oft-quoted advice given to Laertes in Shakespeare's *Hamlet*: "This above all to thine own self be true: And it must follow as the night the day, Thou canst not then be false to any man."

Gandhi's definition of nonviolence was equally broad. It was not just a rejection of violence; it was the positive love for all humanity. "Nonviolence translated 'love' is the supreme law of human beings," he said. "It knows no exception."[5] For Gandhi, violence encompassed all forms of exploitation, including discrimination and poverty. Nonviolence demanded action, requiring work against all forms of exploitation.

There may be other all-encompassing absolute values, but my view is that we should accept the values of truth and nonviolence and move forward to practical tasks.

## WHY TRUTH AND NONVIOLENCE?

Once I had accepted Gandhi's view that absolute values were essential for the conduct of practical affairs, I attempted to establish what living truthfully meant in a practical context. In our personal lives, living truthfully has to be practiced in the context of relationships with other individuals such as family and friends. Similar relationships exist in business with customers, colleagues, employees, shareholders, and society. It became clear to me that much of what we are trying to bring to leadership in business, government, and our communities would fit within the concept of living truthfully.

The quest for quality and truthful advertising, selling, and marketing is living truthfully with respect to our customers. "Walking the talk" means living truthfully with respect to employees and colleagues. Providing

*Gandhi formulated two absolute values: truth and nonviolence. They were linked together, both ends in themselves and means to an end— faces of the same coin.*

*When truth controls action, we move toward complete congruence between words and deeds. This is living truthfully— thinking and acting truthfully.*

the public with accurate information on product risks and safety, environmental impacts, and economic benefits is living truthfully with respect to society. When we do these things from a moral imperative, living truthfully becomes fundamental to our way of living, and we don't give it up because of short-term setbacks—like a decline in sales and profits.

Truth is important for pragmatic reasons as well. With truth as an absolute value, we are committed to seeing things as they really are. Without a true understanding of reality, how can we act with any assurance of success? Acknowledging reality is difficult, especially when it requires change. There is a vested interest in the status quo. When leaders are committed to a course of action, it is difficult for them to accept the reality that they may be wrong. Our national leaders could not acknowledge their errors in Vietnam after they had committed to a strategy of military force. IBM, General Motors, and many other large corporations had to suffer significant financial losses before they acknowledged that their customers' needs had changed and competition had increased. A commitment to truth creates a moral imperative that forces you to acknowledge the data and to take the important first step of recognizing reality.

The practical significance of nonviolence became clear once I understood that violence included exploitation. Protecting the environment, assisting the less fortunate, and putting an end to all forms of discrimination fit within Gandhi's concept of nonviolence. Because we need our entire work force and the talents of everybody, and because we need to leave a habitable environment for the future, a commitment to nonviolence has practical applications. Nonviolence is the moral imperative that directs us to work toward meeting these needs.

## PSEUDO-ABSOLUTE VALUES

We must be on guard against ideology, tradition, and organizational goals masquerading as absolute values. These pseudo-absolute values include national interest, patriotism, group loyalty, capitalism, free markets, and organizational survival. When we turn these into absolute values, we may sacrifice what is fundamental at the altar of what is expedient.

Without the standard of absolute values, pseudo-absolute values can be used to justify violence and repressive acts. Whether it is gang violence in our streets or the horrors that take place in the name of ethnic cleansing, the cause is the same: allegiance to pseudo-absolute values.

*Nonviolence demands action, requiring work against all forms of exploitation.*

*Much of what
we are trying to
bring to leadership
in business,
government, and
our communities
fits within
the concept of
living truthfully.*

Discrimination against racial and religious minorities and against women has been allowed in every part of the world on the basis of pseudo-absolute values — religious dogma, tradition, social custom. But, if we apply the discipline of truth and nonviolence, we see the injustice in these traditions and customs. We see that it is not just an issue of legal rights, but of fundamental values.

Untouchability was, to the vast majority of Hindus, an essential part of Hinduism. But Gandhi, acknowledging the absolute values of truth and nonviolence, could not reconcile the practice even though he was a devout Hindu. At a public meeting in Rangoon in 1929, he said, "Hinduism has got to perish or untouchability has to be rooted out completely."[6] He worked tirelessly, rigorously opposed by tradition-bound Hindus, for the removal of untouchability.

Like most people, I admire loyalty and commitment to causes and leaders. But we know from the bitter lessons of history that loyalty and commitment can be misdirected and can degenerate into policies of exclusivity, discrimination, and repression. Apartheid in South Africa and the persecution of the Jews in Nazi Germany are just two examples of the danger of allegiance to pseudo-absolute values.

In business, loyalty to the organization can cause individuals to support questionable behavior in the treatment of employees, to overlook defects in quality, or to ignore environmental impacts. The enduring safeguard against this kind of misdirected loyalty is a commitment to absolute values.

## The necessity to operationalize absolute values

If asked, we might claim that we subscribe to truth and nonviolence. However, our actions, whether in business, politics, academics, or family life, rarely support this claim because we have not *operationalized* these values.

Operationalizing values transforms them into action. Gandhi operationalized the absolute values of truth and nonviolence when he established his ashram. Adherence to truth and nonviolence and economic self-sufficiency were the objectives of the community. Two of the principles that governed life at the ashram were manual labor and the removal of untouchability. These were operationalized through a requirement that every individual, including Gandhi, had to participate in all the activities necessary for the functioning of the ashram. This included cleaning the latrines—traditionally the work of the untouchables.

*Truth and nonviolence are practical values—we can use them to guide us in our work and personal lives.*

*We have to strive for the ideal; knowing we will not be able to attain perfection is no excuse for not making a commitment.*

If we don't operationalize our ideals, they are often nothing more than slogans. Business talked about product quality for years, but it was not until the measurement of quality was integrated with process design and implementation that improvements in product quality were realized. Measurement resulted in operationalizing quality requirements and made people accountable. Similarly, by operationalizing our values, we take personal responsibility and are willing to be held accountable.

Truth and nonviolence are practical values—we can use them to guide us in our work and personal lives. Complete commitment is the ideal, but any increase in our level of commitment will have a significant positive impact on the quality of leadership. Gandhi's message is that we have to strive for the ideal; knowing we will not be able to attain perfection is no excuse for not making a commitment.

# 2

# ACKNOWLEDGE THE IDEAL

## COMMIT TO THE JOURNEY

Complete adherence to truth and nonviolence is the ideal. To get closer to the ideal, we must translate our beliefs into actions. Doing what we believe is right is what keeps us on the path toward the ideal. This is simple in concept but very difficult to implement. It is easy to believe in something intellectually, but living your beliefs takes a commitment—and that is what staying on the path requires.

In 1904, at the age of thirty-five, Gandhi was living in South Africa and publishing the *Indian Opinion*. He had already simplified his life to a significant extent, but then he read John Ruskin's *Unto This Last* (London: J. M. Dent, 1901)—a book that transformed his life.

*Doing what we believe is right is what keeps us on the path toward the ideal.*

*The object is
to try to
do everything
a little better
tomorrow than it
was done today.
Continuous
improvement
is the path
to a higher standard
of leadership.*

Gandhi derived three principles from Ruskin's book: first, that the good of the individual is contained in the common good; second, that all work has the same value; and third, that the life of labor is the life worth living. "I arose with the dawn," said Gandhi, "ready to reduce these principles to practice."[7]

Gandhi read Ruskin in October; by December he had moved the publication of the *Indian Opinion* to a farm. The work of publishing the newspaper was done after the farm chores were complete. Everyone who lived on the farm had to perform manual labor, and everyone received the same compensation. Gandhi acknowledged the ideal, made the decision to commit to the journey, and translated his commitment into action.

## Evaluating our actions

To move along the path, we must evaluate all of our actions in terms of the absolute values of truth and non-violence and increase the number of actions that adhere to them. The object is to try to do everything a little better tomorrow than it was done today. Continuous improvement is the path to a higher standard of leadership.

In business circles, continuous improvement is already applied to functional areas such as production, marketing, and finance. If we are to stay on the path to a higher standard of leadership, the application of continuous improvement must be expanded to include moral conduct.

The journey toward an ideal never ends; there is always room for improvement. When the ideal seems far away, you should not be discouraged. Think of the distance as a measure of your potential—not of your imperfections. As you gain power and prestige, staying on the path gets more difficult, the impact of your actions is greater, and the temptations of power and privilege are harder to resist. In that case, you may have to increase your commitment.

Even after Gandhi had achieved the status of a world leader, he maintained the most intense effort at striving for the ideal. His secretary, Pyarelal, describes the daily ritual Gandhi performed when he was seventy-seven.

> Daily he held a silent court within himself and called himself to account for the littlest of his little acts. Nothing escaped his scrutiny. He gave himself no quarter. In fact it seemed to onlookers sometimes that he carried his self-examination and self-castigation to the length of being unfair to himself and his closest associates. For instance, it had been an old practice of his to sell by auction, after the evening public prayer, ornaments

*When the ideal seems far away, you should not be discouraged. Think of the distance as a measure of your potential— not of your imperfections.*

*It is not easy to stay on the path; we all need assistance.*

*It is important that we associate with colleagues who share our commitment to be on the path.*

presented to him for the Harijan fund. He had discontinued the practice to save time but it made him feel unhappy to think that he was saving his time at the cost of the Harijans whose trustee he claimed to be, and so he resumed it. Then, on a rainy Saturday evening, prayer was held under a dripping *shamiana* [a large tent] and the auction was omitted as the crowd was much smaller than usual. Afterwards he found fault with himself for it. Did it not betoken lack of faith to fear that the auctions would be low because the crowd was small?[8]

Some may find such dedication to continuous improvement extreme, particularly at such a late stage in one's life. But, if you are trying for "zero defects" in personal conduct, this is the effort that is required.

## STAYING ON THE PATH

It is not easy to stay on the path; we all need assistance. It is important to remember that the majority of Gandhi's time was spent with colleagues from his ashram. These men and women had committed themselves to the same absolute values as Gandhi. It is important that we, too, associate with colleagues who share our commitment to be on the path.

Gandhi used vows to impose the necessary discipline on himself to maintain his commitment, a practice consistent with the tradition in most religions. In practical, everyday life this is equivalent to the "single decision." For example, when an individual makes the decision to never take drugs, that person does not have to go through the decision process every time an opportunity is presented—the decision has already been made. The vegetarian does not look at a menu and decide whether he or she is going to eat meat—the decision has already been made.

We can also make our commitments public. If we do this, we create an external source of discipline to act according to our commitments and focus public attention on the issues we think are important.

In 1920 Gandhi took a vow to wear clothes made only from handwoven handspun cloth, and in 1921 he took a vow to spin every day. To make the spinning vow practical, Gandhi developed the skill to carry on conversations, give interviews, and conduct negotiations while spinning—all of which subjected his commitment to public scrutiny and helped to focus public attention on an issue he felt strongly about.

Evaluating everyday activities is essential to avoid straying from the path. Gandhi, during his travels in

*Evaluating everyday activities is essential to avoid straying from the path.*

*By evaluating*

*our everyday*

*actions,*

*we develop*

*the skill to*

*exercise moral*

*judgment*

*on the*

*bigger issues.*

India by train, traveled third class, which was—and still is—dirty, crowded, and extremely tiring. On one of Gandhi's journeys, a friend offered Mrs. Gandhi the opportunity to use the second class bathroom at a station. Gandhi hesitated but agreed. In evaluating his actions later, Gandhi wrote, "I knew that my wife had no right to avail herself of the second class bathroom, but I ultimately connived at the impropriety. This, I know," he concluded, "does not become a votary of truth."[9]

By evaluating our everyday actions, we develop the skill to exercise moral judgment on the bigger issues. Athletes trying to achieve world-class levels of performance evaluate every aspect of their training, diet, equipment, and previous performances—nothing is too trivial. Likewise, the discipline of evaluation will help us raise the level of our performance as leaders.

# 3

# Develop the Guide That Will Keep You on the Journey

## Commit to Training Your Conscience

Staying on the path of commitment to a single standard of conduct requires that we evaluate our actions in a moral framework. The ability to do this resides in a *trained* conscience—the disciplined, moral reasoning that tells us what we ought to do. According to Gandhi, "It is a quality or state acquired by laborious training."[10] Without a trained conscience, an individual will find it difficult to see the difference between the path of the single standard and the slippery slope of expediency.

A trained conscience is developed through personal reflection. But without a commitment to the truth, personal reflection will result only in rationalization.

The best way to begin is to apply the discipline of truth to everyday statements and actions. When I say I

*Without a trained conscience, an individual will find it difficult to see the difference between the path of the single standard and the slippery slope of expediency.*

lack the time to exercise, is this really true given that I have time to watch television? Perhaps it is just difficult for me to admit that I may be lazy.

Moving to the corporate level, we see tobacco industry executives arguing against a ban on cigarette advertisements and basing their arguments on First Amendment principles of free speech. Would they still argue against it if the ban had the potential of increasing profits? It is often difficult to admit the true basis for one's position. At the national level, President Bush claimed entering the Gulf War was a matter of principle—we had an obligation to repel unprovoked aggression against a defenseless nation. Would we have committed our troops if there had been no oil in Kuwait? Evaluating our actions based on our commitment to the truth can be difficult, but it is necessary if we are to attain a higher standard.

### THE DISCIPLINE OF PERSONAL REFLECTION

Moral growth is not possible without the discipline of regular personal reflection, which is best described as a dialogue with yourself. You formulate questions, seek answers, and evaluate your conduct. I have found that the simplest—but in many ways the most profound—question I can ask myself is, "Did I treat others as I would like to be treated?"

*A trained conscience is developed through personal reflection. But without a commitment to the truth, personal reflection will result only in rationalization.*

Most of us reflect on our actions after we recognize that we have hurt someone or done an injustice. This is certainly a good first step, but it is reactive. We need to be proactive through disciplined and regular personal reflection.

Gandhi demonstrated that personal reflection was a practical endeavor for a political leader. Although action was his domain, his first activity of the day was to spend at least an hour in prayer and meditation. He also led prayers at sundown and had a day of silence every week. He analyzed his actions in the weeklies he edited, *Young India*, *Navajivan*, and *Harijan*, and in his correspondence with colleagues. None of these time-consuming activities diminished the amount of work he put in; indeed, they sustained him. It is not necessary for us to emulate Gandhi's level of reflection, but we can benefit from the direction he set for himself.

I do not believe that disciplined reflection takes time away from work; it sustains the spirit and increases the intensity and quality of work. You may think you do not have enough time. Yet you probably have enough time for meetings with others to discuss policies, procedures, strategy, and your schedule. If you consider personal reflection as a meeting with yourself, it can be scheduled just as your meetings with others are. Once you have set aside time for reflection, you will find that

*Moral growth is not possible without the discipline of regular personal reflection, which is best described as a dialogue with yourself.*

*Disciplined reflection does not take time away from work; it sustains the spirit and increases the intensity and quality of work.*

the discipline of evaluating your actions against the absolute values of truth and nonviolence will begin to permeate all your activities.

The same discipline can be applied to business. Successful business leaders already evaluate everything they do in the context of the strategic imperatives they have set for their organization. But to reach the next level of leadership, such evaluations must be expanded to include moral issues as well. Strategic retreats — off-site meetings where the leadership of an organization reflects on the strategic challenges the company faces — can be expanded to include truthfulness in dealing with customers, employees, and shareholders, and nonviolence by eliminating discrimination against women and minorities or damage to the environment.

# 4

# Reduce Forces That Lead You Astray

## Commit to Reducing Attachments

All of us have attachments. Attachments are relationships, possessions, privileges, and other components of our life we do not want to give up. Some of these attachments, such as family and country, are desirable and have motivated people to do great things. However, we need to acknowledge that attachments such as power, privilege, and possessions, can make it difficult to maintain high moral standards. This fundamental truth is acknowledged by all the great religions of the world. The Buddha identified attachments as one of the causes of suffering. Christ pointed to the extreme difficulty of a rich man entering the Kingdom of Heaven. Even a life of service can have a hidden attachment—the desire for acknowledgment in this world or the next. The recognition

*We need to acknowledge that attachments, such as power, privilege, and possessions, can make it difficult to maintain high moral standards.*

*We know what we ought to do, but our attachments prevent us from doing it, so we condone—and therefore support— bad leadership.*

that attachments are a powerful force in influencing the quality of leadership is the first step to controlling their influence.

Leadership will always have privileges and power associated with it. In many cases a position of leadership also provides the opportunity to acquire wealth. But attachment to privileges, power, and wealth can reduce the standard of leadership. In extreme cases, the preservation of attachments becomes the sole purpose of the leader. The evidence is all around us. We have seen dictators use increasingly repressive measures to maintain their hold on power, and we have seen financiers and securities dealers maintain their high standard of living by misusing the life savings of others.

Attachments can corrupt all levels of an organization. Our need for a job and financial security, for example, may prevent us from speaking out against unethical conduct in the workplace. We know what we ought to do, but our attachments prevent us from doing it, so we condone—and therefore support—bad leadership.

As individuals, we must acknowledge that our personal desire for an ever-increasing standard of living can create conflicts with the attainment of a higher standard of leadership. At some point we have to decide that we have reached an adequate standard of living.

Once we have made that decision, we are more likely to live according to our ideals of truth and nonviolence.

It is possible to have high moral standards and enjoy the material gains that come with success. Gandhi's colleague Jawaharlal Nehru, India's first prime minister, was such an individual, as were Presidents Washington, Lincoln, and Carter and Generals George Marshall, Omar Bradley, and Colin Powell.

In my professional work, I have encountered many successful businessmen and women who have high moral standards. I have noticed two common characteristics in these individuals: they do not measure their success solely by their position in the corporation, and they do not have a desire for ever-increasing wealth. These individuals will not sacrifice their standards of conduct to achieve greater levels of power or more possessions.

## REDUCING ATTACHMENTS

When Gandhi was first drawn into politics, he considered the influence of attachments. He asked himself what he had to do "to remain absolutely untouched by immorality, by untruth, by what is known as political gain."[11] The first requirement, he decided, was to renounce all of his of worldly possessions — voluntary poverty. Gandhi did not achieve this goal in one step. He

*If you establish bounds on your needs and curb your desire for ever-increasing wealth, you remove a major force that could lead to immoral actions.*

> *The first step is
> to understand the
> rationale for the
> various privileges
> you may have
> acquired
> as a leader.
> Every privilege
> should assist
> in meeting
> organizational
> objectives —
> and it is the objective
> you should
> be committed to,
> not the privilege.*

first simplified his life and lowered his standard of living. Later he moved to a commune with his family. He changed from western to Indian dress and then simplified his dress to a loin cloth. It was a gradual process, each step indicating a higher level of commitment. His voluntary poverty identified Gandhi with the people he was leading; his life in terms of material possessions was like theirs. Voluntary poverty is obviously extreme. However, if you establish bounds on your needs and curb your desire for ever-increasing wealth, you remove a major force that could lead to immoral actions.

Once you have acknowledged that attachments to privileges and power can be a hindrance to the achievement of a higher standard of leadership, you can take steps to reduce them.

The first step is to understand the rationale for the various privileges you may have acquired as a leader. Some are necessary for efficiency, some represent the symbolic role of leadership, and others are part of the compensation of the position. An independent evaluation may be necessary to determine which privilege is which. Then, when the organization is looking for inefficiencies and asking for cost reductions through salary cuts and employee layoffs, the privileges of leadership should be examined in the same context and reduced where necessary. Every privilege should assist in meeting organizational objectives—and it is the objective you should be committed to, not the privilege.

Power is also given to individuals in an organization for a purpose—to be used to further the goals and objectives of the organization. The problem occurs when power becomes an attachment and is misused to gain even more power and privilege.

As an individual committed to a higher standard, you must use power within the bounds set by your values, and you have to be willing to risk the power you have to maintain your commitment to your values. I have seen employees refuse—at considerable risk to their careers—to lend their expertise to development projects that they believed would damage the environment or endanger public safety. I know of executives who have left the company rather than implement layoff policies that denied employees their legitimate severance benefits. In some cases such commitment forced the corporation to rethink its policies. But whatever the outcome, these are the kind of individuals who contribute to a higher standard of leadership.

*The problem occurs when power becomes an attachment and is misused to gain even more power and privilege.*

*As an individual committed to a higher standard, you must use power within the bounds set by your values, and you have to be willing to risk the power you have to maintain your commitment to your values.*

Reducing attachments to wealth, power, and privilege is essential to maintaining a commitment to absolute values. As a leader, you can encourage openness and minimize secrecy to provide a source of discipline that will help you reduce these attachments.

# 5

# BE WILLING TO STAND SCRUTINY

## COMMIT TO MINIMIZING SECRECY

A commitment to minimize secrecy forces us to think of the consequences of our actions and provides a discipline that helps us stay on the path. "Secrecy, in my opinion," wrote Gandhi, "is a sin and a symptom of violence, therefore, to be definitely avoided."[12] Gandhi was of the view that individuals and organizations committed to truth and nonviolence could not have secrets.

Gandhi personally lived a life committed to openness. His autobiography, *The Story of My Experiments with Truth*, which covers his life until 1921, is marked by an extraordinary level of candor. He wanted his experiments to help others. He hid nothing because, he wrote, "I am not going either to conceal or understate any ugly things that must be told. I hope to acquaint the

*Secrecy is the enemy of trust and is responsible for much of the distrust that exists between business and society, corporations and customers, management and employees.*

*We share information with people we trust. How can leaders ask for the trust of the people they lead if they are not prepared to share information?*

reader fully with all my faults and errors."[13] Gandhi felt there was no need to extend his autobiography past 1921. "My life from this point onward has been so public that there is hardly anything about it that people do not know."[14]

As Gandhi had no financial assets, there was nothing about his personal finances to hide. Details of his personal life, including the particulars of his daily routine—his diet, baths, massages—were public knowledge. Those who lived with him at his ashram and those who traveled with him could walk into his living quarters unannounced at any time of day or night.

He was as open about his ideas as about his conduct. He did not avoid controversial issues and was always prepared to present his views.

As a society we acknowledge that the conduct of our leaders and organizations in the political arena should be held up to scrutiny. We acknowledge this through our commitment to a free press and to legislation such as the Freedom of Information Act. However, the conduct of our business leaders is rarely reported in any detail even in the business arena, and they are subject to the discipline of full disclosure only in the area of financial performance.

There are important pragmatic reasons for minimizing secrecy in an organization. Leaders who share the strategy, financial performance, and success of the corporation with their employees create a sense of partnership with them. Partners are willing to put in the effort to develop new ideas, to work long hours in emergencies, and to act for the common interest over self-interest, thereby building competitive advantage.

When businesses have to make tradeoffs between economic gain and public health and safety or impacts on the environment, the process is often shrouded in secrecy. Only when there is legal action or an investigation following an environmental accident is the decision process revealed. When we evaluate the process, we often find that, lacking the discipline of openness, the individuals responsible for the decision found it easy to favor short-term economic gain over societal concerns.

The criteria for promotion in a business organization become more secretive and ambiguous the higher the level of the employee. Here secrecy is justified as necessary to evaluate issues of character and temperament. However, secrecy may also be used to exclude people who do not "fit in." If we reduce secrecy and are explicit about our criteria for advancement, we impose a discipline on ourselves that encourages diversity and discourages prejudice.

*A commitment to minimize secrecy forces us to think of the consequences of our actions and provides a discipline that helps us stay on the path.*

*Making it difficult for others to get information is an indirect way to maintain secrecy.*

## Taking responsibility for minimizing secrecy

The majority of the information about business which is now provided to the public has come as a result of legislation and regulation. The predisposition has been to secrecy. Secrecy is the enemy of trust and is responsible for much of the distrust that exists between business and society, corporations and customers, management and employees. For example, it took a great deal of pressure to get publicly owned businesses to disclose details on senior-management compensation. By maintaining secrecy, the leadership appeared unreasonable to those they led.

We share information with people we trust. This is evident in every aspect of our life, from our families and friends to our relationships with our doctors and priests. How can leaders ask for the trust of the people they lead if they are not prepared to share information?

Leadership must have a personal commitment to openness so the people they lead can evaluate their leaders' commitment to the path of a single standard. This needs to be a matter of principle, not something driven by legal and regulatory requirements. Leaders should take personal responsibility for providing the information necessary for the evaluation of their leadership. Making it difficult for others to get information is an indirect way to maintain secrecy.

## THE RESPONSIBILITY OF THOSE
### SEEKING OPENNESS

Those who ask for and evaluate information have a responsibility to use the information in accordance with a commitment to absolute values. Political interest groups often misuse data to advocate a particular position. Many activists use partial data to justify a particular agenda on social and environmental issues. And journalists, in a rush to be first, often don't wait for all the facts before writing the story. If information is taken out of context and used selectively to advocate a particular point of view, the commitment to truth has been violated.

In my own work in analyzing the risks to the public from various developmental projects, I have seen both corporate executives and environmental activists use selected portions of the data to justify extreme positions. These tactics not only confuse the public but also reduce the willingness of people to provide information.

If those who seek openness do not meet their commitment to be truthful, they are equally responsible for the cycle of deception by providing those who have the information the justification for secrecy. Those who ask for information must meet their responsibilities while they ask those who have the information to meet theirs.

*If those who seek openness do not meet their commitment to be truthful, they are equally responsible for the cycle of deception by providing those who have the information the justification for secrecy.*

# 6

# The Essential Quality: Courage

*Each step on the path to a higher standard of leadership takes courage—courage to commit to absolute values and to the universal code of conduct to treat others as ourselves.*

We are all familiar with physical courage: the willingness to risk bodily harm for a noble cause. We honor those who exhibit this quality. We consider them heroic for in extreme cases they are willing to give up their lives for their beliefs. Moral courage is similar: doing what is right and accepting the consequences. In the end, it is moral courage that determines the standard of leadership in the practical arenas of politics, business, academics, and the community.

Gandhi's journey on the path to a higher standard began with a simple, courageous act performed when he was a young lawyer in South Africa. He was traveling in the first class compartment on a train, when the conductor came and asked him to leave because "coloreds"

*It is moral courage that determines the standard of leadership in the practical arenas of politics, business, academics, and the community.*

were not allowed. Gandhi refused, insisting it was his right to travel first class because he had the appropriate ticket. He was forcibly thrown off the train.

At that point, Gandhi felt he had to make a decision. Should he accept color prejudice as the way of life in South Africa and continue his legal work, or should he work to remove the injustice? He made the decision to resist injustice. "I should try, if possible, to root out the disease [color prejudice] and suffer hardships in the process."[15] It became a lifetime commitment. At the time Gandhi had no idea where it would lead; but in the course of human history, few individuals have made decisions with such far-reaching consequences.

Moral courage comes from identification with the intrinsic good in oneself. The greater the identification, the more courage you will have. When you identify yourself with your belief of what is right, you will have the courage to do it. Complete identification makes an individual feel there is no other choice.

When you exercise moral courage and do what you know is right, you may face adversity. Adversity comes in many forms: loss of friends, money, position, popularity, success. In some cases, doing what is right—or not submitting to what you know is wrong—can result in physical pain. Here, moral and physical courage come together.

Continuing his journey by stage coach, Gandhi was forced to demonstrate both. He should have been accommodated inside the coach but was forced to sit outside instead. When the white man in charge of the party decided to smoke, he wanted to ride outside and asked Gandhi to give up his seat and sit on the floor at his feet. Gandhi refused. The man started beating Gandhi, who, as a practitioner of nonviolence, refused to retaliate. "The passengers were witnessing the scene," Gandhi wrote, "the man swearing at me, dragging and belabouring me, and I remaining still."[16] The passengers finally intervened, and the beating stopped. Gandhi was allowed to keep his seat.

Throughout his life Gandhi demonstrated that the way to remove injustice while adhering to nonviolence is to resist by not cooperating. Rosa Parks did the same thing in the United States by refusing to move to the colored section at the back of the bus—an action often credited with launching the civil rights movement. Each of us must have courage and take some individual responsibility for removing injustice if we want to improve the standard of leadership.

Courage is essential to maintain a commitment to the universal code of conduct: to treat others as ourselves. At the simplest level, it may take courage to be a friend. In the business world I have seen executives

*When you exercise moral courage and do what you know is right, you may face adversity. Adversity comes in many forms: loss of friends, money, position, popularity, success.*

*Throughout his
life Gandhi
demonstrated that
the way to
remove injustice
while adhering
to nonviolence is
to resist by not
cooperating.*

shun colleagues who had fallen out of favor. These executives lacked the courage to remain friends because they were afraid for their careers.

To treat all of humanity as oneself requires an extraordinary amount of courage. This is the kind of courage that Gandhi embodied. It is what makes a truly great leader compassionate. Gandhi's work for the untouchables required the courage to go against prevailing custom and power.

When you stand up for what you believe is right, you must have the courage to acknowledge your actions and face the consequences. In the struggle for independence, Indians could be sent to jail for advocating independence and attempting to subvert the "lawful" government. Although Gandhi was sent to jail several times in India, only once was he tried in court. At the trial he told the presiding judge, "I am here therefore to invite and submit to the highest penalty that can be inflicted upon me for what in law is a deliberate crime and what appears to me to be the highest duty of a citizen."[17]

Gandhi, by his own example, inspired others to be courageous—to refuse to submit to unjust laws and to refuse to retreat and retaliate when subjected to violence by law-enforcement personnel. Gandhi also inspired a different kind of courage: the courage to give up the familiar and comfortable and take on new challenges. Many of those who were at the forefront of the struggle for Indian independence gave up lives of ease and comfort to follow Gandhi's example of a simple life. Others defied family and friends to work for religious toleration, to improve conditions in the villages, and to try to eliminate untouchability.

One of the insights that I have gained from Gandhi is that the place to learn about moral courage is in our personal lives—doing what we believe is right and not being subservient to the opinion of others. If we can instill a sense of moral courage in our youth, they will have the confidence to resist those peer pressures that promote drugs, violence, and other destructive behavior.

## COURAGE AND AN INDOMITABLE WILL

With courage a leader wins battles, but it takes indomitable will to win the war. It is the indomitable will of the leader that gives others the confidence that they will overcome. It allows the leader to ask for the impossible and get it.

None of the causes Gandhi espoused and worked for had short-term solutions. His involvement in the struggle for independence from the British lasted over thirty years. His program for the removal of untoucha-

*When you stand up for what you believe is right, you must have the courage to acknowledge your actions and face the consequences.*

*With courage a
leader wins battles,
but it takes
indomitable will
to win the war.
It is the indomitable
will of the leader
that gives others
the confidence
that they
will overcome.*

bility and the self-help programs he started in the villages would never be complete. And his personal struggles to achieve complete adherence to truth and nonviolence lasted until the day he died.

Each step on the path to a higher standard of leadership takes courage—courage to commit to absolute values and to the universal code of conduct to treat others as ourselves. Your courage will serve as a source of inspiration to others and will help those you associate with to achieve a higher standard as well.

Leadership is a way of life, and a courageous life is the life worth living.

# PART 2

# The Spirit

# of Service

Focus On Responsibilities
Not Rights

Emphasize Values-Based
Service

Reconcile Power
With Service

THE SPIRIT
OF SERVICE

Make a Commitment
To Personal Service

Understand The Needs Of The
People You Wish To Serve

Gandhi never held any official position in government, he had no wealth, he commanded no armies — but he could mobilize millions. People were willing to serve with him and for him because his life was devoted to serving them.

Many of us have come to believe that leadership is the attainment of power. But as long as power dominates our thinking about leadership, we cannot move toward a higher standard of leadership. We must place service at the core; for even though power will always be associated with leadership, it has only one legitimate use: service.

The importance of service to leadership has a long history. Ancient monarchs acknowledged that they were in the service of their country and their people — even if their actions were not consistent with this. Modern coronation ceremonies and inaugurations of heads of state all involve the acknowledgment of service to God, country, and the people. Politicians define their role in terms of public service. And service has always been at the core of leadership in the spiritual arena, symbolized at the highest level by Christ washing the feet of His disciples.

Service exists in the context of a relationship. In politics it is between elected officials and their constituents, in academia between teachers and their students,

*If the single standard is the foundation of a higher standard of leadership, the spirit of service is the material with which the structure must be constructed.*

*As long as power dominates our thinking about leadership, we cannot move toward a higher standard of leadership.*

in religion between priests and their congregations, and in interpersonal relationships between loved ones. In business it is between companies and their customers, shareholders, management, and employees.

The ideal is selfless service—you see everybody as yourself and expect no reward. But if you wait until you can serve without any selfish motive, you may wait forever. Gandhi insisted that the best way to attain the ideal was to start on the journey: "If we all refuse to serve, until we attain perfection, there will be no service. The fact is that perfection is attained through service."[18]

Service-oriented leadership does not mean you always do what the people want. Service must be conducted within the bounds of moral values—it must be *truthful* service. If you are committed to truthful service, you may not always tell people what they want to hear. You will have to tell them when you think they are wrong. For this reason truthful service is not always popular. Gandhi, for example, was unrelenting in his criticism of his fellow Indians for their practice of untouchability, their lack of cleanliness, and their tolerance of the extreme poverty and wealth prevalent in India.

In February 1916, Gandhi spoke at the opening of Benares Hindu University. Famous people came from all over India. Maharajahs, in their finery and jewels, sat upon the speakers' platform, but Gandhi first focused his message on the students in the audience.

"I do a great deal of traveling," he said. "I observe the difficulty of third class passengers. But the railway administration is by no means to blame for all their hard lot. We do not know the elementary laws of cleanliness. We spit everywhere on the carriage floor, irrespective of the thought that it is often used as a sleeping space. We do not trouble ourselves as to how to use it; the result is indescribable filth in the compartment."[19]

Later, he turned his attention to the maharajahs. "I compare with the richly bedecked noblemen the millions of the poor," he said. "And I feel like saying to these noblemen, 'There is no salvation for India unless you strip yourself of this jewelry and hold it in trust for your countrymen in India.'"[20]

Gandhi was not afraid to tell the people the unpleasant truths they had to hear to meet their individual responsibilities. Leaders committed to truth and service and not to power and popularity can do this.

As leaders we must build organizations committed to service. We must create an awareness about service, develop a core group who will train others to serve, develop a system to deliver the service, and measure the service to evaluate performance. There is nothing

*Service must be conducted within the bounds of moral values — it must be truthful service. If you are committed to truthful service, you may not always tell people what they want to hear.*

*Gandhi placed before us a higher standard—a standard based on an enduring spirit of personal service founded on individual responsibility and a moral imperative.*

new in these tasks. Many business and volunteer organizations do all these things very well.

As an organizational leader, Gandhi performed all these functions effectively. But he also placed before us a higher standard—a standard based on an enduring spirit of personal service founded on individual responsibility and a moral imperative.

If the single standard is the foundation of a higher standard of leadership, the spirit of service is the material with which the structure must be constructed. In examining the life of Gandhi in the context of today's leadership tasks, I have found five steps that will help make service the centerpiece of leadership:

- Focus on responsibilities
- Emphasize values-based service
- Make a commitment to personal service
- Understand the needs of the people you wish to serve
- Reconcile power with service

To climb these steps requires no special talents, only the desire and commitment to serve.

# 7

# FOCUS ON RESPONSIBILITIES

H.G. Wells once asked for Gandhi's views on a document Wells had co-authored entitled "Rights of Man." Gandhi did not agree with the document's emphasis on rights. He responded with a cable that said, "I suggest the right way. Begin with a charter of duties of man (both D and M capitals) and I promise the rights will follow as spring follows winter."[21]

## SETTING AN EXAMPLE

The emphasis on duties and responsibilities is essential to developing a spirit of service. Most leaders meet the responsibilities related to the functional aspects of their positions very well. The challenge for leaders is to live up to their fundamental responsibility as human beings:

*The challenge for leaders is to live up to their fundamental responsibility as human beings: to treat others as themselves.*

*When we fail
to meet our
responsibilities
to others,
they have to
insist on
their rights.
In some cases,
these rights
have to be
written into laws.*

to treat others as themselves. Leaders need to set an example that will inspire all of us to live up to our individual responsibilities in our families and communities and among our circles of friends.

Gandhi did not ask others to give up the practice of discrimination until he himself had lived among the untouchables and done their work cleaning the latrines. As he wore only handwoven handspun cloth, he could ask others to do the same. He offered nonviolent and truthful resistance to unjust laws, and he willingly went to jail. Consequently, he had the moral authority to ask others to follow.

As a business leader, you ask others to meet their responsibilities to shareholders by generating profits through reducing costs. You must set an example by reducing the costs you directly control. As a CEO, you have the responsibility to ensure that corporate staff costs are below benchmarked values before you ask others to reduce their costs to below industry standards. Whether you are a department head or a supervisor, the principle remains the same: meet your responsibilities before you ask others to meet theirs.

## MEETING RESPONSIBILITIES WHILE INSISTING ON RIGHTS

When we fail to meet our responsibilities to others, they have to insist on their rights. In some cases, these rights have to be written into law. The founders of the United States did not meet their responsibilities to women by denying them the right to vote, nor did they meet their responsibilities to African Americans by allowing slavery. Until recently we did not meet our responsibilities to those with physical disabilities. Each of these groups had to struggle for their rights and get them made into law.

Business leaders insist on their right to be free from government interference in the conduct of their business. However, the majority of government regulations have been put in place because businesses did not meet their responsibility, for example, to protect the environment or the safety of their employees. If business had met its responsibilities initially, it wouldn't have to spend so much effort arguing for its rights today.

Gandhi always believed that those being denied their rights also had to meet their responsibilities. He insisted that his fellow Indians meet their responsibilities to each other by working to end untouchability and poverty. This, he argued, would give them greater moral authority to ask the British for their own rights.

*Whether you are a department head or a supervisor, the principle remains the same: meet your responsibilities before you ask others to meet theirs.*

*As a business leader, you need to make your employees aware of the challenges the business faces. Show them how you are trying to meet your responsibilities, and learn how they are trying to meet theirs.*

Gandhi also insisted that his opponents had a right to courtesy and respect as individuals—to be treated as he would like to be treated. He never forgot the human aspect in any relationship. For Princess (now Queen) Elizabeth's wedding he sent a teacloth that had been handwoven from yarn he had personally spun. When he was in jail in South Africa, he made a pair of sandals for Field Marshall Smuts, who was responsible for putting him in jail.

This same principle can be applied to business relationships. Business leaders participate in labor negotiations, dealings with government regulators, and competition with other businesses. They should always try to treat individuals on the other side with respect and consideration.

Gandhi worked against all forms of exploitation and always tried to convince those who benefited from exploitation to realize that they were not meeting their individual responsibilities as human beings. He felt that this was not only consistent with truth and nonviolence but was the only long-term solution to exploitation. In his campaign for the wearing of handwoven handspun cloth, for example, Gandhi called for a boycott of foreign—primarily British—cloth. This caused a decline in exports from the English mills in Lancashire, resulting in reduced wages and some unemployment. When he went to London for negotiations with the British in 1931, Gandhi insisted on visiting the mills in Lancashire, where he explained to the mill workers that the villagers in India needed to sell their own product to rise above poverty. He pointed out that average unemployment compensation in England was ten times the average Indian's wages. "Do you wish," he asked, "to prosper by stealing the morsel of bread from the mouths of the Indian spinners and weavers and their children?" The workers could see by the way Gandhi lived that his concern for the poor was genuine, and they showed him a great deal of affection. Gandhi was deeply moved and said he would remember those days until "the end of his earthly existence."[22]

As a business leader, you need to make your employees aware of the challenges the business faces. Show them how you are trying to meet your responsibilities, and learn how they are trying to meet theirs. Then you may be able to find ways to help each other.

Gandhi demonstrated that meeting one's responsibilities in no way diminishes the intensity of the struggle for justice. It intensifies it, since it is all put in the same context: living up to our responsibilities as human beings.

> *A society driven by responsibilities is oriented toward service, acknowledging other points of view, compromise, and progress — whereas a society driven by rights is oriented toward acquisition, confrontation, and advocacy.*

*In business the highest level of motivation occurs when all employees are driven by a sense of personal responsibility to do their work to the best of their ability.*

## Meeting responsibilities creates benefits for all

There are pragmatic reasons for all of us to focus on our responsibilities rather than our rights. A society driven by responsibilities is oriented toward service, acknowledging other points of view, compromise, and progress—whereas a society driven by rights is oriented toward acquisition, confrontation, and advocacy. If we meet our responsibility to treat others as ourselves, the fabric of society does not have to be threatened in the struggle to achieve rights.

In business the highest level of motivation occurs when all employees are driven by a sense of personal responsibility to do their work to the best of their ability. When this occurs, there is less need for supervision and there is more efficiency and greater productivity.

Today, however, the trend in all aspects of society seems to be toward rights and not responsibilities. The concept of meeting obligations and responsibilities because it is the right thing to do seems to be declining. We cannot expect to reach a higher standard of leadership if we do not recognize that meeting our responsibilities should be a way of life, not a way of gaining rewards. It should have its foundation in the family, where parents and elders set an example for the children who will be the leaders of the future. It needs to be reinforced in the community and workplace where you, as a leader, set an example by focusing on your responsibilities and calling on others to meet theirs.

*We cannot expect to reach a higher standard of leadership if we do not recognize that meeting our responsibilities should be a way of life, not a way of gaining rewards.*

# 8

# EMPHASIZE VALUES-BASED SERVICE

The service that Gandhi espoused was based on a moral imperative: you serve your fellow human being because it is the right thing to do. The rewards for such values-based service are personal fulfillment and a sense of satisfaction.

The service most organizations deliver is designed to meet organizational objectives: it is based on policy. Policy-based service relies on effectiveness and external motivation. The rewards are advancement, money, and acclaim. When your commitment is based on policies, it is easy to reduce service when conditions change or short-term results are not favorable. An enduring spirit

*The service that Gandhi espoused was based on a moral imperative: you serve your fellow human being because it is the right thing to do.*

*For Gandhi,
all acts of service
had to pass the
tests of truth
and nonviolence,
and service to
any group
had to benefit
all of humanity.*

of service, one that will lead to a higher standard of leadership, requires a values-based approach.

## SERVICE TO ALL

Gandhi, believing in the oneness of humanity, placed service within the context of service to all. "Personal service," he wrote, "when it merges into universal service is the only service worth doing."[23] For Gandhi, all acts of service had to pass the tests of truth and nonviolence, and service to any group had to benefit all of humanity.

In 1946 it was clear that Gandhi's political vision of a free, united India was not going to prevail. There were ongoing political negotiations about the partition of India and the creation of Pakistan, and there was a threat of violence between Hindus and Muslims. The violence finally erupted in the province of Bengal, where Muslims subjected Hindus to violence, murder, rape, and looting. Hindus retaliated in the province of Bihar, subjecting Muslims to similar treatment. Many of Gandhi's political colleagues advocated using force to quell the riots, even though they had committed themselves to nonviolence during the struggle for independence. Under the new circumstances, they felt violence would be a more efficient policy. Gandhi disagreed. He immediately left the scene of political power and went to the riot-torn areas to comfort those who had suffered and to counsel those who had committed violence. He served all the people, and as his service was based on absolute values, it would not be compromised because the circumstances had changed.

Service to any group—shareholders, customers, employees, or society—should be done in the context of service to all. If you deliver superior customer service or increase shareholder wealth by mistreating employees, or provide excessive employee and management benefits and compensation by making the business uncompetitive, the business will suffer in the long term.

The CEO of a major Japanese corporation effectively explained this principle in his orientation speech to new employees. He would draw a circle on a board to represent the income of the company and divide it into segments, each segment representing the share of a constituency—such as management, labor, customers, and shareholders—and then explain how each constituency used to try to increase the size of its segment at the expense of another. He told them that he believed the purpose of each individual in the corporation was to increase the size of the whole circle, which could only be achieved by serving all constituencies. Then he would erase all the lines that divided the circle into segments.

*Service to any group— shareholders, customers, employees, or society— should be done in the context of service to all.*

> *In business
> it is not possible
> to make service
> a moral imperative
> because of
> the system
> of rewards and
> compensation.
> Service can,
> however,
> become a
> cultural value
> or tradition
> in the business.*

In serving many constituencies, there will always be short-term inequities. However, when the people are convinced that the leader's commitment to service is enduring and based on values, they will be more tolerant of the short-term inequities.

## MAKING SERVICE A TRADITION

In business it is not possible to make service a moral imperative because of the system of rewards and compensation. Service can, however, become a cultural value or tradition in the business. When this happens, service becomes the expected thing to do.

This is one area in which there has been great progress in American business. Companies have given front-line employees the training, tools, and responsibility to provide good service, and they have acknowledged individuals and groups who provided superior service. Thus they have created a tradition. The Ritz Carlton hotel chain, L. L. Bean, Federal Express, ServiceMaster, Lexus dealerships, and many other companies have demonstrated that providing great service to customers is the path to business success. When a company becomes known for its tradition of service, it attracts and keeps employees who have the desire to be of service, and the tradition is maintained.

An enduring spirit of service, driven by values, will continue to give purpose to your life even when you are no longer in a policy-making position. President Carter, for example, left office with his popularity at a very low level, but his commitment to service based on his religious beliefs has given him a lasting purpose. He now helps build homes for the poor through Habitat for Humanity and works on mediating conflicts in developing countries. Without much fanfare, he has developed a life of service, based on his values, that has far outlasted the political power he once had. As a result, he has gained the respect of people everywhere.

*An enduring spirit of service, driven by values, will continue to give purpose to your life even when you are no longer in a policy-making position.*

**9**

# MAKE A COMMITMENT TO PERSONAL SERVICE

When Gandhi left the scene of political power in 1946 to visit the riot-torn areas of India, he was seventy-seven years old. His schedule was brutal. He worked fifteen to eighteen hours a day and walked 116 miles in sixty days to comfort victims in forty-six villages. Here, in the midst of unspeakable savagery, was a frail individual with the courage to fulfill his commitment to truth and nonviolence. He asked those who had suffered to forgive, and, at the same time, asked those who perpetuated the violence to repent.

After touring the villages in Bengal on foot, he went to Bihar, Calcutta, and Delhi with the same mission. These years of service and suffering were considered by many to be Gandhi's greatest achievement. Through

*You and I do not have to wait for a great cause to make a commitment to personal service. It can start with those nearest to us: our family and friends.*

*Commitment to personal service requires performing the service through direct contact with the individuals receiving the service.*

his commitment to personal service, Gandhi brought stability to the province of Bengal and the city of Calcutta at the boundary of India and Pakistan while a force of fifty thousand soldiers could not do the same in the boundary province of Punjab. Lord Mountbatten, the Viceroy of India, referred to Gandhi as his "one man boundary force."

## MAKING A COMMITMENT

You and I do not have to wait for a great cause to make a commitment to personal service. It can start with those nearest to us: our family and friends. Once we feel the satisfaction of living up to our small commitments, we will do more.

In the context of political and business leadership, commitment to personal service requires performing the service through direct contact with the individuals receiving the service. This means "front line" work with customers, employees, shareholders, and suppliers.

Many business leaders have already embraced the concept of performing personal service. I have observed executives who spend time taking customer orders and listening to customer complaints; others go on the road with sales and service representatives to call on customers; and some respond to shareholder and employee concerns personally. The challenge is to perform personal service on a regular basis.

Everyone in the organization, irrespective of position, can commit to one personal act of service every day. The issue is not lack of time but lack of spirit. It is a question of priorities. Surely you can cut down on some unnecessary meetings or your political and social activities to find time to engage in direct service to your employees, customers, shareholders, or community. The simple step of doing one act of personal service every day will keep you in direct contact with the overarching work of leadership: service.

Gandhi's commitment to personal service began in 1897, when he was twenty-eight. He was living in Durban, South Africa at the time and had been thinking of how he might be of service to his fellow human beings. When a leper came to his door, Gandhi took him in, dressed his wounds, and started to look after him. Gandhi soon realized, however, that he could not do this indefinitely in his existing circumstances. He had brought his family with him from India and had established a legal practice. He placed the leper in a government hospital and rearranged his legal work so that he could devote two hours a day at a local charitable hospital for indentured laborers where he presented patient

*Everyone in the organization, irrespective of position, can commit to one personal act of service every day.*

> *It is not
> how much we give,
> but how much of
> what we have
> that we give
> that determines
> the level of our
> commitment.*

complaints to the doctor and dispensed medicines. "This work," Gandhi wrote, "brought me some peace."[24] This was the beginning of a life of service.

There are different levels of commitment to personal service. Some individuals, within the constraints of their other obligations, devote their energies to help others with no reward; others receive minimal compensation in return. These are the two groups of people we should revere. Unfortunately, many of us tend to honor those who give money, at no hardship to themselves, rather than those who actually provide service. If we would honor those who gave of themselves instead, we would increase the level of commitment to service in society as a whole. It is not how much we give, but how much of what we have that we give that determines the level of our commitment.

### RESPECTING THE COMMITMENT OF OTHERS

A major focus of Gandhi's life was to improve the lives of the poor who lived in the villages of India. Conditions in the villages were primitive, and literacy and knowledge of public-health principles minimal. Gandhi had walked in the villages, talked to the people, and seen the conditions for himself. He knew what had to be done, and he called on the more fortunate in India to devote some time assisting the villagers improve their conditions.

However, he still felt he did not understand the difficulties of living and serving in a village. He had been "talking and giving advice on village work without personally coming to grips with the difficulties of village work."[25] So, in 1936, at the age of sixty-five, Gandhi—India's most prominent leader—went to live in a typical Indian village with no running water, electricity, or paved roads. This was more than a gesture; it was a commitment.

When you call on others to serve, you should understand what you are asking for. A leader committed to service spends the effort to understand the difficulties of implementation. If you do this, those implementing your decisions will be more likely to support you because you will have demonstrated your respect for their commitment to service. When you combine your personal commitment with respect for the commitment of others, you will initiate a compounding effect that will create a commitment to service throughout the organization.

*When you combine your personal commitment with respect for the commitment of others, you will initiate a compounding effect that will create a commitment to service throughout the organization.*

# 10

# Understand the Needs of the People You Wish to Serve

Some months after Gandhi's departure from Bengal, a poor, old man from a remote village came to see one of the individuals who was carrying on Gandhi's work and asked when Gandhi would be returning. On receiving a vague reply, the old man said, "If *he* were here, he at least would have cared for us. Who else is there to feel our woes?"[26]

To understand the needs of the people you serve, as Gandhi did, you must get personally involved, speaking and listening to the people, observing and sharing their experiences. Look below the surface and identify the hidden or unarticulated needs that others cannot see and create a bond with those you are trying to serve. Opinion polls, employee surveys, and market research

*Look below the surface and identify the hidden or unarticulated needs that others cannot see and create a bond with those you are trying to serve.*

*Feel,
not just
intellectualize,
the needs
of the people.*

can help you understand what people need. To achieve a higher standard of leadership, you must go further. *Feel,* not just intellectualize, the needs of the people whether you are in business, politics, or academia. This is what Gandhi did, and this is why a poor, old man in a remote village believed that Gandhi, a world leader, cared about him and understood his plight.

## Personal observation

Personal observation and a commitment to the truth allow a leader to see things as they really are: to understand the true needs of the people. Politicians must spend time listening to their constituents, business executives and managers must meet with employees and customers, and those who design and deliver goods and services must listen to consumers. Unfortunately, it is too easy to neglect this task or to rely on others to do it for you. But you must spend time among the people to get a true picture. If the people do not see your personal commitment to serve them, they are not likely to share with you information about their deepest needs.

When Gandhi returned to India from South Africa in 1916, he spent a year traveling around India and Burma by train. In 1927 he again toured India for ten months to promote his handwoven handspun cloth program. In 1933 and 1934 he traveled throughout India again for seven months campaigning against untouchability. When he traveled by train, Gandhi rode in third class among the poorest Indians. He spent time with those who lived in poverty—visiting them where they lived, in their villages and huts—and gained first-hand knowledge of their lives. He dressed like them and arrived on foot—in humility and the spirit of service.

Through his personal contact with the people, Gandhi identified and personalized the real problems of Indian society: the practice of untouchability, the lack of interest in sanitation and hygiene, religious intolerance, discrimination against women, and the exploitation of Indians by Indians. Of all the political leaders in India at the time, Gandhi more than anybody saw independence in a broad context that had to include freedom from fear, discrimination, and poverty.

Gandhi's personal observations gave him another clear insight: Indians had lost their self-esteem. How else could a tiny country such as Britain rule a country like India for almost two hundred years? Gandhi saw the need for Indians to stop assuming that Britain was somehow culturally superior and to develop an appreciation for their own language, culture, and heritage.

*Personal observation and a commitment to the truth allow a leader to see things as they really are: to understand the true needs of the people.*

*Every step
we take—
no matter
how small—
to understand
the needs of
the people we
strive to serve will
increase our bond
with them and
move us in the
direction of
a higher standard
of leadership.*

Personal observation and a commitment to the truth allowed—perhaps forced—Gandhi to see reality.

We can examine failures in business and the errors of government policy; we can argue about faulty strategy and tactics. But if we look deeper, we are likely to see one common factor: the leaders did not see reality. In the 1970s the automobile industry did not understand the customer or appreciate Japanese competition. During the Vietnam War, the United States did not accept that local Vietnamese support for America had declined. The leaders were not in the field with the people they were supposed to serve. Nor did they have a sufficient commitment to the truth to acknowledge the data they had. To succeed, you must understand the needs of the people—you must commit yourself to personal observation and interpret what you see with a commitment to the truth.

## IDENTIFY WITH THE PEOPLE

Gandhi went beyond personal observation by sharing the experiences of the people he tried to serve. He lived among the untouchables and did their work. He lived among the poor villagers. When he went to Calcutta to calm the violence there, he lived among the Muslims in an abandoned house.

Shared experience creates the deepest understanding and the most lasting bonds of attachment. We see this among family members, coworkers, teammates, and soldiers. The people of India, especially the poor, felt this bond with Gandhi and recognized in him an individual who truly cared about their well-being. They saw the embodiment of all their religious teachings. But this was not some ancient, mythological figure; here was somebody *living* the talk.

The Nobel Laureate Rabindranath Tagore captured the essence of Gandhi's hold on the poor: "He stopped at the threshold of the huts of the thousands of dispossessed, dressed like one of their own. He spoke to them in their own language. Here was living truth at last, and not only quotations from books. For this reason the *Mahatma* [great soul], the name given to him by the people of India, is his real name. Who else has felt like him that all Indians are his own flesh and blood?"[27]

Gandhi set a standard that few of us may be able to attain. Nevertheless there are many small steps we can take to move along the path. In business, sharing experience means putting yourself in the customer's shoes, being a customer to your own company to gain the experience of how customers are treated, or working with employees on specific projects to understand their

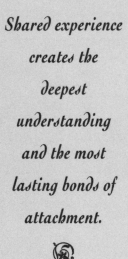

*Shared experience creates the deepest understanding and the most lasting bonds of attachment.*

difficulties. Politicians could consider living with low-income constituents to understand the realities of being poor. There are many opportunities for sharing experiences, but it has to be done with humility and a spirit of service. Every step we take — no matter how small — to understand the needs of the people we strive to serve will increase our bond with them and move us in the direction of a higher standard of leadership.

*There are many opportunities for sharing experiences, but it has to be done with humility and a spirit of service.*

# 11

# RECONCILE POWER WITH SERVICE

Gandhi had power, but he had none of the means we usually associate with power: wealth, official position, military might. His power was based solely on the willingness of people to follow his lead. They were willing to serve him because his life was devoted to serving them.

One of the great challenges of leadership is to develop harmony between service and the power that is necessary for the exercise of leadership. The ideal is power derived solely from service and used only for service. This is the power that lasts through the ages. It is the power that influences the spirit of humanity.

In any organizational context—from business and

*One of the great challenges of leadership is to develop harmony between service and the power that is necessary for the exercise of leadership.*

*You can exercise power through control or through service. Control motivates people through their attachments. Service motivates people through their sense of personal obligation and a moral imperative.*

politics to academia and family—there is power associated with positions in the organization. The measure of this power is your decision-making authority. In business this authority resides in setting the direction of the business, the assignment of work, the allocation of resources, and the advancement of careers.

Power provides the authority to convince people to act in a way that moves the business, or any organization, toward its objectives. You can exercise power through control or through service. Control motivates people through their attachments. In business it is exercised by supervising employees, determining their compensation, and offering job security. Service motivates people through their sense of personal obligation and a moral imperative. It is exercised by setting an example and creating the moral authority to ask others to take individual responsibility.

The greatest source of power in any organization is personal power: the character, courage, determination, knowledge, and skill of the individual members of the organization. To move the organization toward its objectives, we need to harness this power, not emasculate it. When leadership exercises its control through demagoguery and fear—exemplified in the extreme case by

Hitler and Stalin—individuals surrender their personal power to the leader. The organization then suffers from the lack of spirit, creativity, and commitment these individuals may have provided. By balancing control with service, the leader can exercise decision-making authority without diminishing the personal power of the individual.

## RECONCILING POWER WITH SERVICE

Gandhi proposed the concept of *trusteeship* to reconcile the issues of power, wealth, and talent with service. He spent his life as a trustee for humanity. His talents, power, and influence were all used for the benefit of humanity, not for any personal gain.

Such an extraordinary level of commitment is not necessary to live a life of service. However, there is an important lesson to be learned from Gandhi's example. Power is given to you by others. It is not yours; it is in trust with you and it is a great responsibility. Power is to be used for the benefit of those whose trustee you are.

Many business executives think of themselves as trustees of the capital provided by the shareholders. But business leaders must also think of themselves as trustees of the labor provided by employees, of the

*The greatest source of power in any organization is personal power: the character, courage, determination, knowledge, and skill of the individual members of the organization.*

*Power is given to you by others. It is not yours; it is in trust with you and it is a great responsibility. Power is to be used for the benefit of those whose trustee you are.*

resources they use to provide goods and services, of the confidence that customers have in the product, and of the relationship the company has with the community and the environment.

Leadership is not a technique. It is a way of life — from the family to the highest office in the land. The power and privilege that come with leadership have the potential to corrupt a leader. But trusteeship allows a leader to reconcile power with the spirit of service.

# PART 3

# Decisions and Actions Bounded by Moral Principles

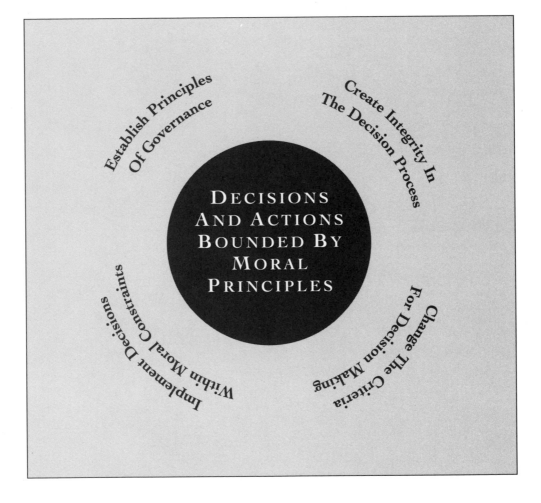

Gandhi was a man of action. He implemented every idea he espoused, but every action he took had to pass the test of his commitment to truth and nonviolence. Whether it was a protest movement on a national scale or a personal decision concerned with his health or diet, Gandhi evaluated every decision against the criteria of truth and nonviolence.

Actions define leadership, and decisions are the precursors to action. Decide where you want to go: this is your goal. Decide how you are going to get there: this is your strategy. Then do what you said you would do. You must monitor the results and adapt to changing circumstances. But to attain a higher standard of leadership you must also consider the moral dimension in all decisions and actions.

Including the moral dimension requires evaluating decisions and actions against the absolute values of truth and nonviolence and the universal code of conduct: to treat others as ourselves. We must remind ourselves that nonviolence means the positive love of humanity and the absence of exploitation. We must be explicit in our commitment to consider these as decision-making criteria in the business and political arenas.

Too often the moral dimension is ignored when we make business or political decisions. But these decisions

*The majority of our life is spent in work. If our work lacks a moral dimension, is it not likely that the moral content of the rest of our life will decline?*

*Including the moral dimension in our decisions can be difficult. But decisions that affect the lives of other people should not be easy.*

have an impact on other people and therefore have a moral dimension. We cannot escape this reality. Nor can we escape the fact that including the moral dimension in our decisions can be difficult. But decisions that affect the lives of other people should not be easy.

The majority of our life is spent in work. If our work lacks a moral dimension, is it not likely that the moral content of the rest of our life will decline? As parents, will not the moral influence on our children decline, and will not the moral fiber of our society—of which business and politics is a major component—decay?

Fundamental to Gandhi's thinking was his belief in the goodness of the individual. He believed that individuals *want* to work for the common good. That is why he called on people to make sacrifices to achieve independence and uplift the poor and why he appealed to the sense of honor and conscience of those who opposed him. As a result, many heeded his call for sacrifice, and his opponents, though skeptical at first, always treated him with courtesy and respect.

Including the moral dimension in our decisions and actions will bring out the best in us as well. It will make us think and act beyond narrowly defined business and political interests and give meaning and purpose to our working lives.

After examining how Gandhi maintained his commitment to truth and nonviolence in his decisions and actions, I have identified four steps that will help others bring the moral dimension to their roles as leaders in society:

- Establish principles of governance
- Create integrity in the decision process
- Change the criteria for decision making
- Implement decisions within moral constraints

These four steps not only create the framework for leaders to continue on the path of a higher standard of leadership, they also provide a foundation for the organization to support those who have chosen to be on the path.

*Including the moral dimension in our decisions and actions will bring out the best in us. It will make us think and act beyond narrowly defined business and political interests and give meaning and purpose to our working lives.*

# 12

# Establish Principles of Governance

Principles of governance establish the bounds and constraints on the goals we set and the actions we take to achieve these goals. At a national-policy level, our principles of governance are embodied in the Constitution. Whatever our objective, whether it is reducing crime or stimulating the economy, our actions must be conducted within the bounds set by the Constitution.

Based on the absolute values of truth and nonviolence and the universal code of conduct, I propose the following three principles of governance which, if adhered to, will help keep us on the path to a higher standard:

- Include moral criteria in evaluating decisions and actions

*Principles of governance establish the bounds and constraints on the goals we set and the actions we take to achieve these goals.*

> *The moral direction set by our decisions and actions determines the nature of the society in which we live.*
>
> ®

- Acknowledge the fusion of ends and means
- Respect the intrinsic good in every individual

### INCLUDE MORAL CRITERIA IN EVALUATING DECISIONS AND ACTIONS

At a personal level, Gandhi's commitment was to a moral life. He defined personal achievement in terms of his adherence to the moral criteria of truth and nonviolence. Economic considerations had little or no place. Gandhi's example asks us, as individuals with career goals, to include a commitment to a moral life by considering moral criteria in pursuit of our goals. We must ask ourselves what we are willing to do to be successful.

As a society, we are being provided with an increasing array of options driven by science and technology, from advances in genetics to advances in telecommunications and weaponry. Now, more than ever before, our principles of governance must include moral principles.

The moral direction set by our decisions and actions determines the nature of the society in which we live. To enjoy the economic gains we have all worked so hard to achieve, we must live in a civilized society. And we cannot expect to create a civilized society unless we bring a moral dimension to our work environments.

In business we must evaluate our decisions and

actions on the basis of moral criteria just as we do on economic criteria. Every company makes a commitment to be a profitable company. To also make a commitment to be a moral company requires that decisions and actions be evaluated on the basis of moral criteria. The moral criteria for business include truthfulness between the company and its customers and shareholders and between the management and employees. They also include nonviolence by eliminating the exploitation of employees, society, and the environment. It is not necessary to commit to perfection, but to progress. To do that, we need to monitor our progress by evaluating our performance against moral criteria.

## ACKNOWLEDGE THE FUSION OF ENDS AND MEANS

We usually think of goals and the means to achieve them in a sequential manner. This in itself is not the problem. It is when we do not apply the same standards to both the ends and the means that we are in danger of lowering our standard of leadership. The values of truth and nonviolence must apply to both.

Gandhi was not willing to compromise on means, however noble the cause. In leading the struggle for Indian independence from the British, for example, he

*Every company makes a commitment to be a profitable company. To also make a commitment to be a moral company requires that decisions and actions be evaluated on the basis of moral criteria.*

*It is when we do not apply the same standards to both the end and the means that we are in danger of lowering our standard of leadership. The values of truth and nonviolence must apply to both.*

refused to participate in or condone deception and violence even when it was motivated by patriotism. Gandhi was not just concerned with physical violence; he was equally concerned with violence done to the human spirit through exploitation, humiliation, and fear. He believed that if the independence movement used violent and untruthful means to achieve its goal, the society it created would be predisposed to accept the efficacy of untruth and violence as a means of achieving its goals. As we see the increasing violence around us, we are beginning to recognize the truth of Gandhi's message.

Our own society has a long history of using and glamorizing violence and deceptive practices to achieve results. In the business world, some companies encourage violence to the spirit by rewarding executives who achieve economic goals by humiliating people and motivating them through fear. If we encourage violence in the workplace, how can we stop violence in our society?

In business, the evaluation of performance and the system of rewards is primarily based on achieving economic goals such as revenues, profitability, sales quotas, and cost targets. This has often resulted in many untruthful practices—unconfirmed orders being booked as revenues, deceptive sales practices to meet individual sales quotas, revenue and expense shifting at the end of the year—all to gain rewards.

Such deceptive practices in business and in politics, and the exploitation of women, minorities, and the environment create the cynicism and hopelessness that promote—but never justify—violence. As leaders in business we must all work against these practices to have credibility in calling for an end to the physical violence that is becoming prevalent in society. To do this we must apply the test of absolute values to both ends and means.

## RESPECT THE INDIVIDUAL

Gandhi believed in the intrinsic good in every individual—the universality of humankind. He asked individuals to search for the truth that was within them and to act in accordance with their conscience. He devoted a great deal of his life trying to convince people to acknowledge the good in others, to reject differences based on caste, religion, and social position, and to work for the welfare of all.

Gandhi not only appealed to the best in those who followed him, but also to the best in those who opposed him. Whether the struggle was for independence, the abolition of untouchability, or communal harmony, Gandhi appealed to the conscience and morality of his opponents. He sought to convert them, not to coerce them.

*We must ask ourselves what we are willing to do to be successful.*

*In business, respect for the individual means acknowledging that every individual wants to do good work and to contribute to the success of the organization.*

In business, respect for the individual means acknowledging that every individual wants to do good work and to contribute to the success of the organization. This is a significant departure from the idea that people do not want to work and must be constantly monitored and supervised. Respect for the individual means that the leadership provides its employees with the tools and the training to do their work well, in addition to some choices as to how they do their jobs: for the people doing the work can often find ways to do it better. Each individual should also be able to evaluate how what he or she does contributes to the success of the organization. When employees feel competent, have choices, and know they are making a contribution, they enjoy their work and are at their most productive level.

A business that appeals to the best in their employees will ask people in different departments, groups, and divisions to subordinate their particular group interests and work for the good of the whole. The leadership must provide the system and support for people to work for the common good, creating a spirit of community—without which competing group interests could threaten the survival of the whole. From major corporations, such as Coca-Cola and General Electric, to small entrepreneurial companies, the concept of the seamless or boundaryless organization is now being hailed as the organization of the future.

Organizational changes are not enough. A spirit of community has to be created for the whole to be greater than the sum of its parts. The role of leadership in creating this spirit is to acknowledge and respect the contribution of each individual to the success of the business. As a business leader, this respect must be present in all your interactions with your employees.

Corporations are now beginning to cooperate with each other on social issues, and, through public-private partnerships, programs are being created to protect the environment, improve educational standards, and develop better ways of delivering health care. There are opportunities to appeal to the best in people in all fields of endeavor.

With these three principles of governance — inclusion of moral criteria in evaluating decisions and actions, the fusion of ends and means, and respect for the individual — you have established the platform from which you will lead. This is more than leadership style; it is the *substance* of your leadership.

*Organizational changes are not enough. A spirit of community has to be created for the whole to be greater than the sum of its parts.*

## 13

# CREATE INTEGRITY IN THE DECISION PROCESS

In business, speed is a competitive weapon—quick and effective decision making is essential to success. Therefore, a primary objective in the design of a decision-making process is timeliness. But if we are to move to a higher standard of leadership, timeliness is not enough. The decision process must have, and be perceived to have, integrity—not integrity based on compliance with legal and regulatory requirements, but integrity based on moral principles.

Why do we need integrity in the process? In a free society, support for a decision is dependent on confidence in the integrity of the process. Without this support, decisions cannot be effectively implemented.

*In a free society, support for a decision is dependent on confidence in the integrity of the process.*

> *To create integrity in the decision process, the first requirement is that individuals who participate in the process have integrity.*

To create integrity in the decision process, the first requirement is that individuals who participate in the process have integrity. At the same time, the process must support and reinforce the integrity of all those who participate.

Just as the integrity of individual decisions is governed by personal values, the decision process must be governed by process values. These are logical extensions to our commitment to a single standard: truthfulness in gathering and interpreting data and openness about the process. All those who participate in the decision-making process have a responsibility to live up to these values, but it is the leadership that must set the tone. If we are to be effective in gaining support for our decisions, we have to create a decision process that has, and is perceived to have, integrity.

## TRUTH IN GATHERING AND INTERPRETING DATA

Gandhi's work in Champaran on behalf of the indigo farmers is illustrative of his commitment to truth in gathering and interpreting data. Champaran was a rural district in Bihar, a province in northeast India. Much of the land was cultivated by tenant farmers for European planters. The peasants were required to plant a portion of their land with indigo, a very profitable cash crop, and turn it over to their landlords as rent. However, when synthetic indigo became available in the world markets, natural indigo was no longer a good cash crop, so the planters converted the indigo requirement into cash payments or increased rents but still required the peasants to grow indigo on what was often their best land. The financial obligations that the peasants had to bear created a feudal system in which everything the peasants owned was subject to taxation and confiscation by the planters.

Gandhi was approached by a local agriculturalist, Rajkumar Shukla, who knew of Gandhi's civil rights work on behalf of Indians living in South Africa, for help in remedying the injustices in Champaran. This was 1916. Gandhi had only just returned from South Africa and knew nothing about the plantations in Champaran. He had no idea that the little packets of indigo he had seen in the markets had been produced through such hardship to thousands of people.

In 1917 Gandhi went to Champaran. His first task was to collect data. He recruited a group of individuals who had made a commitment to a simple life in the performance of service to interview the villagers. Gandhi wanted them to personally observe the living conditions

*Just as the integrity of individual decisions is governed by personal values, the decision process must be governed by process values.*

*Truth in data and opinions promotes better decision making. When we see the situation for what it really is, the decision is forged on the anvil of truthful debate.*

of the peasants. They were instructed to approach the villagers with humility and in a spirit of service. Only then, Gandhi told them, could they expect the villagers to open up and tell them their true concerns.

Gandhi also visited the villages himself and saw inadequate sanitation, illiteracy, and poor health care — none of which were caused solely by the indigo requirement. He met with the planters and local British officials to make sure he heard all points of view, and he did not take a position until he had collected all the facts. Then, with his band of volunteers (some of whom were lawyers), he prepared and presented more than ten thousand depositions specifying the injustices against the peasants. There were negotiations with the planters and the government, and a commission was appointed to investigate and to recommend actions. As a result, the system of indigo planting was abolished, and the government paid the peasants partial compensation for past injustices.

It would have been easy to blame the planters for all the problems Gandhi saw at Champaran, but that would have violated Gandhi's commitment to the truth. The planters were clearly responsible for the indigo problem, but Gandhi recognized that the literacy and sanitation problems had to be solved by the villagers themselves with help from their countrymen. Therefore Gandhi confined his discussion with the planters and British officials to the indigo problem and set up programs to improve sanitation, health care, and literacy independently. Gandhi's willingness to face all the facts and address each of them provided evidence of his true intent: service to the peasants. Thus, both the peasants and the government had confidence in the integrity of his process.

Leaders often take an advocacy position and neglect facts that do not support their position. But, by acknowledging the truth in the collection and interpretation of data, leaders not only see issues in a broader context, they create integrity in the process.

As a leader, you may not wish to espouse an unpopular view, reveal harsh realities, or go against the prevailing wisdom because you don't want to endanger your leadership position. However, you bear a great responsibility. If you set the direction, analysis and support will appear throughout the organization *even if you are wrong*. Those who are not in positions of power will find it difficult to disagree—to be truthful—because they fear for their careers and their futures.

Truthful interpretation of data requires courage. Individuals with specialized knowledge and information must have the courage to state their opinions even when

*By acknowledging the truth in the collection and interpretation of data, leaders not only see issues in a broader context, they create integrity in the process.*

*Openness can be defeated by complexity. Processes that are technically open can be so difficult to understand that in reality they are secret.*

it conflicts with the preferences of the leaders. Leaders need the courage to change direction when the data warrants it.

Truth in data and opinions promotes better decision making. When we acknowledge all the facts, including our own deficiencies, we have the basis for effective decision making. When the force of moral persuasion is on our side, we can appeal to the conscience of others. When we see the situation for what it really is, the decision is forged on the anvil of truthful debate.

## OPENNESS IN THE DECISION PROCESS

A leader committed to a single standard is committed to minimizing secrecy and to promoting openness in the decision process. Openness is an essential aid to the personal integrity of leaders. Not only does it impose discipline on the process by revealing any favors done for special interests, it also reveals the intent of special interests to sacrifice the common good for personal gain.

Openness can be defeated by complexity. Processes that are technically open can be so difficult to understand that in reality they are secret. Some of our legislative decision making falls into this category. The process is subject to public evaluation, but the complexity of the process through hearings, committee meetings, and last-minute deals and compromises makes the process extremely difficult to evaluate. If we cannot explain the process in simple terms, we are asking for people to have faith. And who among us has the stature to ask for faith?

If we are to reduce the influence of special interests on the decision-making process, we must first acknowledge who the special interests are. They are us. They are the companies we work for, the communities we live in, and the organizations we belong to, whether the American Association of Retired Persons or the National Rifle Association. *We* are the special interests we complain about.

In principle, there is nothing wrong with people organizing to advocate their point of view. Unfortunately, we are often asked to exert our influence through financial contributions instead of truthful debate, and we often put our interest above the common good.

In business, personal career advancement is a special interest, as are resource allocations to various departments or groups. What we must guard against is making decisions or trying to influence decisions in a way that benefits our special interests over the interests of the business as a whole. Openness in the decision process will help us achieve this.

> *If we are to reduce the influence of special interests on the decision-making process, we must first acknowledge who the special interests are. They are us.*

*Openness allows all who are impacted to evaluate the decision. It creates a sense of integrity about the process — it promotes trust.*

We all share the responsibility to maintain openness in the decision process with our leaders. As individuals we must be careful not to emphasize our special interests over the common good; otherwise we will discourage our leaders from maintaining openness in the decision process. As leaders we must set an example by being willing to explain the decision process and by encouraging others to do the same. Openness allows all who are impacted to evaluate the decision. It creates a sense of integrity about the process — it promotes trust.

# 14

# Change the Criteria for Decision Making

A large body of literature and a great deal of expertise are available on decision making—on how people make and how they should make decisions—and are used with skill by leaders in business and politics. But it is not the techniques of decision making that need changing—it is the criteria. We need to include truth and nonviolence, the universal code of conduct (to treat others as ourselves), and the spirit of service.

When one of his workers asked for help in decision making, Gandhi told him, "I will give you a talisman. Whenever you are in doubt, or when the self becomes too much with you, apply the following test. Recall the face of the poorest and the weakest man whom you may have seen, and ask yourself, if the step you contemplate is

*"Recall the face of the poorest and the weakest man whom you may have seen, and ask yourself, if the step you contemplate is going to be of any use to him."*

> *When we include moral criteria in business, we have made a commitment to do what is right. This will require tradeoffs, which might include sacrificing some short-term economic gains.*

going to be of any use to *him*. Will he gain anything by it? Will it restore him to a control over his own life and destiny? In other words, will it lead to *swaraj* [freedom] for the hungry and spiritually starved millions? Then you will find your doubts and yourself melting away."[28]

Gandhi's criteria embodied a spirit of service that we can apply in business to all stakeholders and in politics to all constituencies.

When we include moral criteria in business, we have made a commitment to do what is right. This will require tradeoffs, which might include sacrificing some short-term economic gains. To do this effectively, we must incorporate absolute values and the universal code of conduct in establishing goals and crafting strategy.

## ESTABLISHING GOALS

We generally agree that goals in business and government and in our personal lives should be bounded by moral standards and legal constraints. Yet very few of us take active steps to develop a moral life. For some reason we are reluctant to have goals based on moral principles. Are we afraid we will not measure up? This happens all the time with economic goals and it does not deter us. Perhaps we are afraid to measure our performance on morally derived goals because of what it would tell us about who we are as human beings. Perhaps we are afraid to look into that mirror. But, to proceed to a higher level of leadership, we have to overcome this fear and include morally derived goals in our businesses and our lives.

Gandhi's goal for his ashrams was that they support themselves economically while the inhabitants advanced spiritually. To achieve this goal, he established a "spiritual balance sheet" as an adjunct to a financial balance sheet to measure progress on the spiritual dimension. "Everybody should draw up such a balance sheet for himself or herself and all of us together for the Ashram as a whole," he wrote. "If we do not follow this practice, we would become spiritually bankrupt."[29]

With the spiritual balance sheet Gandhi not only created a very high standard of moral conduct in the ashram, he also developed a group of extremely disciplined and committed individuals. In all the difficult tasks Gandhi undertook—when complete adherence to truth and nonviolence was essential—he could call on individuals who had been trained in the ashram to lead others in nonviolent resistance.

Individuals and groups make moral progress when the leadership establishes goals and sets an example. For example, over the last twenty-five years many

*Individuals and groups make moral progress when the leadership establishes goals and sets an example.*

*In addition to establishing goals with a moral dimension, we must also develop measures of performance.*

businesses have moved from neglecting to actively protecting the environment. Most major corporations now have corporate goals that require them to minimize the negative impact their activities have on the environment. These corporations are on the path to a higher standard.

In addition to establishing goals with a moral dimension, we must also develop measures of performance. In business we have already done this by establishing specific measurable performance goals in areas such as finance, marketing, production, and product development. We have come from general goal statements of growth and profitability to detailed measurements of market share and profitability by product and market segment. Quality goals have been converted to detailed measurements on component and performance specifications. We now take this for granted, but it took a great deal of effort and many years to progress from general statements of desirable performance to specific measures of performance. The new challenge for leadership is to do the same with absolute values, deriving specific objectives and measures of performance.

If, for example, truth is one of the moral principles we subscribe to, we need to derive goals based on this principle and ways to measures our performance.

Looking at the relationship a business has with its customers, we can easily identify three areas where truth is important: truth in advertising, truth in packaging, and truth in personal selling. Consider our commitment to total quality where we try for "zero defects" in product quality. Why can't we set similar standards for "zero defects" in "truth with customers"? We can form independent panels with the authority to correct misstatements and misrepresentations to evaluate proposed advertising, packaging, and selling, and determine if there is a departure from truthfulness. We can apply the same approach to eliminate discrimination and sexual harassment and to increase product safety.

I can already hear the objection that it costs too much. This was the same objection we heard when total-quality principles were introduced. Now we know that doing it right the first time is much more cost-effective than correcting the problem after the fact. Some may object that it will be hard to develop quantifiable measures for moral goals. But we already know that measurement can include subjective estimates: most incentive plans and performance-appraisal systems require subjective judgment, and these are used throughout business and government.

Society is interconnected. Deceptive practices in

> *Consider our commitment to total quality where we try for "zero defects" in product quality. Why can't we set similar standards for "zero defects" in "truth with customers"?*

> *Society is interconnected. Deceptive practices in business and government may not appear to injure anyone, but they permeate the system and reduce the moral standards of society.*

business and government may not appear to injure anyone, but they permeate the system and reduce the moral standards of society. When we try to correct immoral behavior, we are reminded that "everybody does it." It is time we took a stand and set specific goals based on moral principles.

## INCLUDING MORAL PRINCIPLES IN CRAFTING EFFECTIVE STRATEGY

In 1930 Gandhi was given authority by the Indian National Congress, the major political organization agitating for Indian independence, to start a civil-disobedience campaign. To Gandhi, civil disobedience was a last resort. As an individual committed to truth and nonviolence, he wanted to give his opponents, the British, an opportunity for a negotiated solution. Therefore, Gandhi proposed an eleven-point program that, if the British accepted, would remove the need for immediate civil disobedience and allow negotiations to continue for independence.

The eleven points Gandhi selected affected Indians in their daily lives. He did not ask the British to withdraw, nor did he mention independence. He gave the British a practical alternative to immediate independence and withdrawal. But they did not accept Gandhi's proposed program. Gandhi now felt he was morally justified in launching civil disobedience.

Gandhi believed that any law he planned to break — or encouraged others to break — had to be considered unjust in terms of conscience. Additionally, all forms of protest had to be nonviolent. A strategy that could not conform to these moral standards would not be used. After carefully considering many options, Gandhi chose to base his campaign on the abolition of the salt-tax law.

The government had a monopoly on the manufacture of salt and prohibited private individuals from manufacturing salt even for their own consumption. In addition, the price of salt included a tax that provided revenue for the British administration (one of the most extravagant in the world at that time) and had a severe impact on the poorest Indians in particular.

Most politicians could not understand Gandhi's choice of the salt tax as the basis for the struggle, but the choice was brilliant. Because it required no technology, anybody could participate in the protest by making their own salt; because of the government's monopoly, the protest posed no threat to Indian business interests; and because everybody needed and used salt, the protest had an emotional appeal.

Gandhi selected a group of about eighty individuals

*When your strategy includes a commitment to moral principles, it commands the respect of your opponents — decreasing, if not eliminating, the ill will that can exist.*

*Incorporating moral values in strategy motivates people at every level in every type of organization — business, political, and academic — because of its appeal to what is basic in all of us: our desire to do what we know is right.*

committed to and trained in nonviolence to march with him two hundred and forty miles from his ashram in Ahmedabad to Dandi on the west coast where they would purposely break the law by extracting salt from the sea. He also gave out the call that when he reached Dandi and broke the law, everybody who had the opportunity should do the same by making salt and selling it. He created a huge sense of anticipation, and for an entire month, the national and international press followed the small band of nonviolent marchers taking on the greatest empire in the history of the world.

When Gandhi reached Dandi, people throughout India began making their own salt — eventually turning this into the largest protest movement Gandhi ever led. He was arrested one month later and sent to jail, and within a few months another one hundred thousand Indians had been arrested. When Gandhi was released from jail in January 1931, the Viceroy negotiated an agreement with him that allowed Indians on the coast, at least, to manufacture their own salt. It was the first time that the Viceroy, the representative of British power, had negotiated with an Indian on equal terms, and it was a major step toward the ultimate goal of independence. Gandhi's strategy was built on moral principles, and that is where its strength lay. Strict nonviolence had been observed, which took away the government's military advantage and maintained India's moral advantage. He also relied heavily on one of India's greatest competitive advantages: sheer numbers of people. This was one of the great strategic confrontations in history, and all the advantages were with Gandhi.

When your strategy includes a commitment to moral principles, it commands the respect of your opponents—decreasing, if not eliminating, the ill will that can exist. Because Gandhi insisted on nonviolence throughout the struggle for independence, the British did not retaliate with mass repression and ultimately left India with a general absence of bitterness. Both countries benefited as a result.

Incorporating moral values in strategy motivates people at every level in every type of organization—business, political, and academic—because of its appeal to what is basic in all of us: our desire to do what we know is right. As a leader, applying moral principles to decision making will also allow you to appeal to the conscience of your customers, employees, and shareholders. Customers have shown a preference for companies that superimpose moral standards of conduct on quality products and service. In addition, employees feel proud to be with a company that has high moral

> *Employees feel proud to be with a company that has high moral standards, and this is a source of individual motivation and increased productivity.*

*If businesses include the moral dimension in their strategy and create an advantage for themselves, others will have to follow and society as a whole will benefit.*

standards, and this is a source of individual motivation and increased productivity. Consequently, many companies are now prospering because of their environmental policies, or because they provide child care, or because they hire and promote qualified minorities. The moral dimension adds competitive value, and the business or political program that has both an economic and moral dimension to its strategy will have the advantage.

A commitment to the truth also provides the best defense against two of the most common errors in strategic decision making: rush to judgment and groupthink. A rush to judgment occurs when you take the first available solution without considering all the facts. Groupthink occurs when people do not state their convictions, primarily because they want to agree with the dominant view. There is no greater defense against these errors than a commitment to the truth exemplified by the leader. If you wait for all the facts before making a judgment and always state your convictions, you will encourage others to do the same.

There is yet another reason to change the criteria for decision making: the benefits accrue to all of society. When the Japanese automobile and electronic companies introduced the concept of total quality to products for the mass market, customers became more conscious of quality and value—they expected more and demanded more. American companies were forced to follow, and the overall quality of products and services improved as a result. It is the same with moral standards. If businesses include the moral dimension in their strategy and create an advantage for themselves, others will have to follow and society as a whole will benefit.

Including and adhering to moral criteria in developing strategy does not require additional education or technical skills. It requires qualities of the spirit that are in all of us irrespective of race, gender, creed, or origin. It allows the widest participation so that we can each take individual responsibility to bring moral standards to decision making in all aspects of society.

*Including and adhering to moral criteria in developing strategy does not require additional education or technical skills. It requires qualities of the spirit that are in all of us irrespective of race, gender, creed, or origin.*

# 15

# Implement Decisions Within Moral Constraints

*If you are not committed to adhering to absolute values in implementation, the entire fabric of a higher standard of leadership breaks down.*

If you are not committed to adhering to absolute values in implementation, the entire fabric of a higher standard of leadership breaks down. It is in this last step that most leaders falter.

It is easy to be true to your principles when you are adhering to your values and getting the results you want. The challenge occurs when sales are increasing but selling techniques lack integrity, profits are increasing but regulations are being circumvented in the process, and productivity gains are being achieved but some managers have created a climate of fear. You are achieving economic gains, but you are using immoral means. This is when your commitment to absolute values is

*To maintain a higher standard of leadership during implementation, a commitment to evaluate actions against absolute values has to cascade through the entire organization.*

tested. If you are not getting the results you want, people may bring you ideas that compromise on moral principles to achieve the results. In some cases people will take the initiative and take the necessary steps to get the results. You have to reject such ideas and stop these actions.

To maintain a higher standard of leadership during implementation, a commitment to evaluate actions against absolute values has to cascade through the entire organization. This commitment has to exist at three levels: leaders, teams, and individuals—with each level supporting the other two.

### LEADERSHIP TAKING A STAND

In December 1920, the Indian National Congress, the leading Indian political organization, had adopted peaceful noncooperation with the British as a policy to undermine British rule and to move the country toward independence. Gandhi was the driving force in developing this policy. In November 1921, during the visit of the Prince of Wales (who became Edward VIII), there were calls for peaceful boycotts of receptions for him. However, there was some violence by Indians against some of those who had participated in the welcome, which distressed Gandhi greatly. He spoke out publicly against the violence and fasted for five days as penance.

A month later, the Indian National Congress gave Gandhi complete authority to lead a massive, national, nonviolent resistance movement. In two states peasants decided not to pay taxes as part of the resistance. If this spread throughout the country, the British government would soon be unable to govern, and the empire would be brought down. It appeared that the means for independence was at hand.

Unfortunately, there were still some outbreaks of violence and when, on February 4, 1922, a group of demonstrators killed twenty-two policemen in Chauri Chaura, Gandhi was convinced that the people were not ready to conduct the resistance movement with a commitment to nonviolence, and he called off the program. He not only reversed a potentially successful course of action, he was also opposed by almost all of his colleagues and put his entire political career at risk by this decision. Massive nonviolent resistance was not launched again until 1930.

Independence was a noble goal, but any action to achieve it had to meet Gandhi's test of truth and nonviolence. He would not sacrifice moral principles for political gain.

Gandhi was equally strict in matters that impacted him on a personal level. In May 1915, five months after

*If you do not have the spirit of nonviolence, you create a strategic vulnerability: not only will you be equated with the very people you oppose, you will not appeal to the best in others.*

*Team members need to be evaluated on their commitment to moral principles so they can work together to bring the moral dimension to decisions and actions.*

his return to India from South Africa, Gandhi established an ashram on the outskirts of the city of Ahmedabad. This was before Gandhi became a national political leader, and he had not yet begun his national campaign against untouchability. Twenty-five individuals attempted to live as a family in the ashram with Gandhi providing spiritual leadership. As it was not yet self-sufficient, donations were accepted to pay for services provided to students and guests.

The ashram had been in existence for only a few months when an untouchable family applied for admission and was accepted. When people in the outside community became aware of untouchables living in the ashram, all financial support ceased. Other members of the ashram were subjected to insults when they went to draw water from the community well, and there was a threat that ashram members would be denied access to all public facilities such as shops and public transport. There were even some in the ashram, including Gandhi's wife, who thought living with untouchables was a sin and refused to associate with them. Gandhi held firm to his principles even when it appeared that his wife, who later accepted his position, may leave the ashram. When the ashram ran out of funds, Gandhi decided to move it to the untouchables' quarter on the outskirts of

Ahmedabad where he and the other members would live on what they could earn by manual labor. But before this became necessary, an anonymous donor provided funds for the ashram to continue. Nevertheless Gandhi had shown that he was willing to make the sacrifices necessary to adhere to his moral principles.

In all his campaigns against exploitation and injustice, Gandhi always tried to adhere to his commitment to truth and nonviolence. As a result, he was always able to maintain the force of moral persuasion on his side.

Many individuals may be willing to take a stand and the causes they stand for—peace, environmental protection, free speech—may be noble, but maintaining the spirit of nonviolence is often difficult. Many of those demonstrating for noble causes are discourteous, vilify their opponents, and are often filled with hate. Demonstrations may be "peaceful," but they are not nonviolent. In practical terms, if you do not have the spirit of nonviolence, you create a strategic vulnerability: not only will you be equated with the very people you oppose, you will not appeal to the best in others, and the number of people from whom you can draw support will decline. During the 1960s, the students and demonstrators taking over faculty offices, interfering with the rights of others to pursue an education, and dishonoring soldiers who

*When team members share a commitment to moral standards in addition to business strategy, the team has the greatest level of alignment.*

*Many individuals may be willing to take a stand and the causes they stand for — peace, environmental protection, free speech — may be noble, but maintaining the spirit of nonviolence is often difficult.*

were doing their duty as they saw it alienated a lot of people who otherwise supported their cause. In addition, these images often were used by their opponents to discredit their cause and to continue the very policies the students and demonstrators were against.

### BRINGING THE MORAL DIMENSION TO TEAMS

Teams — groups of people working together to reach specific objectives — are widely used in business and government and have proven effective over a wide range of situations. Team members are usually selected for their technical and managerial expertise and their ability to work together, but they also need to be evaluated on their commitment to moral principles so they can work together to bring the moral dimension to decisions and actions.

The team Gandhi put together to collect data from the villagers at Champaran had technical expertise — they were lawyers and educators — but they also had to commit themselves to serving the villagers. Gandhi could rely on them to go to the villages in a spirit of service and to be truthful in their reporting of all the information they gathered. For the Dandi Salt March, Gandhi's major campaign of nonviolent resistance after the Chauri Chaura incident, Gandhi personally selected the individuals on the basis of their commitment to nonviolence.

When team members share a commitment to moral standards in addition to business strategy, the team has the greatest level of alignment. The team members do not have to compartmentalize their lives; what is good for business does not conflict with what is good for the spirit. They do not have to separate being good human beings from being good businessmen or women; they can devote their minds and spirits to their work. This is the highest level of teamwork.

### EMPOWERMENT WITH A MORAL DIMENSION

To bring the moral dimension to all levels in the organization, it is necessary to bring the moral dimension to individual actions. One of the most significant management concepts to evolve in the last few years has been to give decision-making responsibility to individuals throughout the business. This concept, known as *empowerment,* has two essential aspects: responsibility with the authority to make decisions, and accountability against promised results. We now know that empowerment combined with the appropriate skills has the potential of capturing efficiency and creating success.

Until now, empowerment has been confined primarily to making business decisions. It is time to expand its effectiveness and scope by making every

*To bring the moral dimension to all levels in the organization, it is necessary to bring the moral dimension to individual actions.*

*Taking a stand during implementation is often difficult: the decision has been made and things are moving forward, and then you call things to a halt or ask for a change in direction.*

member of the organization feel empowered to act in accordance with the moral principles that the corporation has adopted and to challenge corporate decision making when it does not conform with those principles. There is an analogy from the quality movement. In some automobile companies, each individual on the production line has the responsibility and the authority to stop the process if that individual sees a defect in the product. We need all of our employees to feel a similar sense of responsibility about moral principles.

Taking a stand during implementation is often difficult: the decision has been made and things are moving forward, and then you call things to a halt or ask for a change in direction. You risk criticism and missing time deadlines. However, if you don't call a halt, the consequences could be worse. Many of us can often look back at such situations and ask, "Why didn't somebody say something?" But we are the people who should have said or done something. We have an obligation to call attention to discrimination, unethical behavior, and intimidation. We have to do it not for personal gain, but to improve the system. If we don't, then we are participants in this immoral behavior.

At the most fundamental level, all conduct is individual. So, when you bring the moral dimension to individual actions, you bring integrity to the entire work environment. Therefore, leaders must set an example. They must also acknowledge and support those individuals who are willing to act in accordance with moral principles and to embrace the absolute values of truth and nonviolence and the universal code of conduct: to treat others as ourselves.

*At the most fundamental level, all conduct is individual. So, when you bring the moral dimension to individual actions, you bring integrity to the entire work environment.*

# Conclusion:
# Taking up the Challenge

We are all leaders. Each one of us is setting an example for someone else, and each one of us has a responsibility to shape the future as we wish it to be. But we must have ideals to guide our conduct if we are to make a positive difference.

Truth and nonviolence, the universal code of conduct (to treat others as ourselves), and the value of a life of service are as valid today as they were in Gandhi's time. These ideals and commitments are global in their application and universal in their truth. They do not belong to any ideology, race, or culture; they belong to all of us.

To reach a higher standard of leadership, we do not have to make dramatic changes in our lives—there is a lot we can do without changing our standard of living. We can be truthful in dealing with others and ourselves. We can commit to not exploiting others or misusing our natural resources. And we can try to treat others as we would like to be treated. When we, as

*Each one of us is setting an example for someone else, and each one of us has a responsibility to shape the future as we wish it to be.*

> *Your life is your message. Leadership by example is not only the most pervasive but also the most enduring form of leadership.*

individuals, live according to these principles, we set standards for our leaders to live up to. When those in leadership positions act on these principles, they set an example for all who follow. One person can make a difference. *You* can make a difference. And you *will* make a difference when you adhere to a single standard of conduct, adopt a spirit of service, and act within a moral framework.

Your life is your message. Leadership by example is not only the most pervasive but also the most enduring form of leadership. And because the world is becoming more interconnected, standards of leadership have an impact that extend around the globe. Now, as never before, a higher standard of leadership will serve us all.

# A Brief History of Gandhi

Mohandas Karamchand Gandhi was born into a well-established family on October 2, 1869 and was married according to traditional Hindu custom at thirteen to Kasturbai. He had a traditional Indian upbringing, showed no special gifts at school, and did not stand out in any way.

In 1888, Gandhi left for England to study law at the Inner Temple in London and was called to the Bar in 1891. While in England he became associated with the London Theosophical Society and the London Vegetarian Society. He increased his knowledge of Hinduism and familiarized himself with Buddhism and Christianity. When he returned to India in 1891, he tried to establish a law practice but was unsuccessful. Consequently, he accepted an offer to become a legal advisor to Dada Abdullah & Company and spent the next twenty-one years (1893–1914) living and working in South Africa. During this time he returned to India only twice.

While he lived in South Africa, Gandhi—through a process of introspection and study—developed most of the concepts and principles that would govern the rest of his life. He committed himself to nonviolence and to seeking the truth, took vows of voluntary poverty and chastity, and embraced the concept of service and the idea that all forms of labor are equal. He also developed and tried the concept of *satyagraha* (truth force or passive resistance) in the political arena.

Gandhi worked on behalf of Indians living in South Africa who were subjected to discrimination and anti-Asiatic legislation including a law requiring Indians to carry registration certificates at all times; a law that only gave legal status to marriages that had been solemnized according to Christian rites; and an annual "head tax" that was prohibitive for most Indian laborers. Gandhi — hoping to fill the jails of the union and thus expose the immorality of the anti-Indian laws — called on his fellow Indians to join him in nonviolent resistance. Between January 1908 and May 1909, Gandhi was arrested and sentenced to prison three times, and between November 6 and December 18, 1913, he was arrested and released another three times. On January 22, 1914, Gandhi negotiated an agreement with General Jan Christiaan Smuts, the Minister of the Interior, that validated all Indian marriages and abolished the head tax.

Gandhi left South Africa and arrived in India in January 1915 when he was forty-five. For the next thirty-three years, he worked to achieve Indian independence from British rule, to remove untouchability, to revive village industries — especially spinning — as a means to alleviate poverty, to increase self-esteem among the poor, to promote education, and to create communal harmony among peoples of the various religions, primarily Hindus and Muslims. Gandhi founded his own organizations to eradicate untouchability and to promote village industries. He edited, at various times, three news weeklies: *Navajivan*, *Young India*, and *Harijan*. These gave him the means to express his views.

During the struggle for independence, Gandhi was arrested and sent to prison five times—the last time in August 1942 when he was seventy-three years old. He never spent more than two years in jail at any one time, often being released because of ill health. His wife, Kasturbai, died while in prison with Gandhi in 1944.

Gandhi traveled extensively in India by train and on foot—often for months at a time—and knew more about the conditions of the poor than any other politician. He also visited the neighboring countries of Ceylon (Sri Lanka) and Burma. He went to England in 1931 to represent India at the Round Table Conference where he meet with British leaders to explain the reasons for Indian independence. He visited Europe on his way back home and never left India again.

Gandhi received visitors from all over the world and corresponded with individuals in all walks of life. He completed his autobiography, *The Story of My Experiments with Truth*, in 1929, which covered his life through 1920. He never felt the need to extend his autobiography since his life had no secrets and his thoughts had all been expressed in public through his speeches and writings. His correspondence, articles, and other writings comprise more than ninety volumes.

In 1946, as Indian independence drew near, the harmony between Hindus and Muslims that he had worked so hard for all his life evaporated, and violence broke out. Gandhi worked tirelessly to bring peace, walking among the people in the afflicted areas and preaching the gospel of nonviolence, forgiveness, and repentance. When India achieved independence in August 1947, Gandhi did not participate in the celebration. Instead he continued his work to end the violence in the cities and villages of Bengal and Bihar.

Gandhi went to Delhi, the capital, in late 1947, and on January 13, 1948, he began a fast for communal harmony. The fast ended on January 18, 1948, when the killing and violence abated.

Gandhi's pleas for harmony created bitterness among certain radical Hindu elements and, while going to his evening prayer meeting on January 30, 1948, Gandhi was felled by an assassin's bullet fired at close range. He died as he had lived: in the service of his people and with the name of God on his lips.

# Suggested Readings

There have been more books written about Gandhi than anybody except the founders of the world's great religions. What I have provided here is a short list that represents my personal preferences.

For a general biographical overview, I suggest:

Fisher, Louis, *The Life of Mahatma Gandhi.* New York: Harper & Brothers, 1950.

Shirer, William Laurence, *Gandhi: A Memoir.* New York: Simon & Schuster, 1979.

Easwaran, Eknath, *Gandhi the Man.* Petaluma: Nilgiri Press, 1978.

For a more detailed biography, I recommend:

Tendulkar, D. G., *Mahatma.* Eight volumes. New edition. New Delhi: Publications Division of the Government of India, 1961.

Pyarelal, *Mahatma Gandhi: The Last Phase.* Ahmedabad: Navajivan; Volume I, 1956, Volume II, 1958.

Pyarelal, *Mahatma Gandhi: The Early Phase.* Ahmedabad: Navajivan, 1965.

To gain an insight into Gandhi's personal development, his autobiography is must reading although it ends in 1921:

Gandhi, M. K., *The Story of My Experiments with Truth: An Autobiography* (translated by Mahadev Desai). Boston: Beacon Press, 1957.

To understand Gandhi's philosophy and his moral and political thought, there are the masterly and elegant expositions of Professor Raghavan Iyer:

Iyer, Raghavan N., *The Moral and Political Thought of Mahatma Gandhi.* Second edition. Santa Barbara: Concord Grove Press, 1983.

Iyer, Raghavan N. editor, *The Moral and Political Writings of Mahatma Gandhi.* Oxford: Clarendon Press, Volumes I, II, 1986, Volume III, 1987.

To get a historian's perspective, the following works by Professor Judith Brown are comprehensive:

Brown, Judith M., *Gandhi's Rise to Power: Indian Politics 1915–1922.* Cambridge: Cambridge University Press, 1972.

Brown, Judith M., *Gandhi and Civil Disobedience: The Mahatma in Indian Politics 1928–1934.* Cambridge: Cambridge University Press, 1972.

Brown, Judith M., *Gandhi: Prisoner of Hope.* New Haven: Yale University Press, 1989.

It is difficult, if not impossible, to appreciate Gandhi without a minimum understanding of Hinduism. The following brief texts provide the reader with a concise yet reasonably comprehensive view:

Zaehner, R. C., *Hinduism.* Oxford: Oxford University Press, 1962.

Radhakrishnan, Sarvepalli, *The Hindu View of Life.* London: Mandala Books, 1927; Unwin Paperbacks, 1980.

The Bhagavadgita and The Principal Upaniṣads had a profound influence on Gandhi. The translations and commentary suggested below have extensive introductions and place these texts within a western context:

Radhakrishnan, Sarvepalli, *The Bhagavadgita*. Great Britain: George Allen & Unwin Ltd., 1948. First Indian reprint: George Allen & Unwin (India) Private Ltd., 1971. Sixth Indian reprint: Blackie & Son Publishers Private Ltd., 1979.

Radhakrishnan, Sarvepalli, *The Principal Upaniṣads*. London: George Allen & Unwin Ltd., 1953. New York: Humanities Press Inc., 1978. [Gandhi was particularly influenced by the Isa Upaniṣad, verse 1, p. 567.]

An excellent source of additional books on Hinduism is the Vedanta Society of Southern California, 1946 Vedanta Place, Hollywood, CA 90068.

# NOTES

1. Nehru, Jawaharlal. *An Autobiography* (The Bodley Head Ltd., London, 1989), 129.

2. Gandhi, M. K. Interview with Denton J. Brooks, *The Hindu*, June 15, 1947. In Iyer, R. N., ed. *The Moral and Political Writings of Mahatma Gandhi* (Clarendon Press, Oxford, 1986), I:37–38.

3. Gandhi, M. K. Talk with a Christian Missionary, *Harijan*, September 22, 1946. In Iyer, R. N., ed. *The Moral and Political Writings of Mahatma Gandhi* (Clarendon Press, Oxford, 1986), I:395.

4. Gandhi, M. K. Letter to Narandas Gandhi, 1930. In Iyer, R. N., ed. *The Moral and Political Writings of Mahatma Gandhi* (Clarendon Press, Oxford, 1986), II:163.

5. Gandhi, M. K. Letter to William Q. Lash, January 1945. In Iyer, R. N., ed. *The Moral and Political Writings of Mahatma Gandhi* (Clarendon Press, Oxford, 1986), II:341.

6. Gandhi, M. K. *Young India*, 4 April 1929. In Iyer, R. N., ed. *The Moral and Political Writings of Mahatma Gandhi* (Clarendon Press, Oxford, 1986), I:59.

7. Gandhi, M. K. *The Story of My Experiments with Truth: An Autobiography* (Beacon Press, Boston, 1957), 299.

8. Pyarelal. *Mahatma Gandhi, Last Phase* (Ahmedabad, Navajivan, 1956), I:347.

9. Gandhi, M. K. *The Story of My Experiments with Truth: An Autobiography* (Beacon Press, Boston, 1957), 385.

10. Gandhi, M. K. "Under Conscience's Cover," *Young India*, 21 August 1924. In Iyer, R. N., ed. *The Moral and Political Writings of Mahatma Gandhi* (Clarendon Press, Oxford, 1986), II:125.

11. Gandhi, M. K. Speech at Guildhouse Church, *The Guildhouse*, September 1931. In Iyer, R. N., ed. *The Moral and Political Writings of Mahatma Gandhi* (Clarendon Press, Oxford, 1986), I:382.

12. Gandhi, M. K. Letter to Amanda Babu Chowdhary, *Glimpses of Gandhi's Life*, 74–75. In Iyer, R. N., ed. *The Moral and Political Writings of Mahatma Gandhi* (Clarendon Press, Oxford, 1986), II:438.

13. Gandhi, M. K. *The Story of My Experiments with Truth: An Autobiography* (Beacon Press, Boston, 1957), 503.

14. Ibid.

15. Ibid., 112.

16. Ibid., 114.

17. Tendulkar, D. G. *Mahatma* (Publication Division of the Government of India, New Delhi, 1961), II:97.

18. Gandhi, M. K. Letter to K. Santanam, 1926. In Iyer, R. N., ed. *The Moral and Political Writings of Mahatma Gandhi* (Clarendon Press, Oxford, 1986), II:37–38.

19. Tendulkar, D. G. *Mahatma* (Publication Division of the Government of India, New Delhi, 1961), I:182.

20. Ibid.

21. Gandhi, M. K. Cable to H. G. Wells, *The Hindustan Times*, April 16, 1940. In Iyer, R. N., ed. *The Moral and Political Writings of Mahatma Gandhi* (Clarendon Press, Oxford, 1987), III:492.

22. Tendulkar, D. G. *Mahatma* (Publication Division of the Government of India, New Delhi, 1961), III:123.

23. Gandhi, M. K. Letter to Amrit Kau, 1947. In Iyer, R. N., ed. *The Moral and Political Writings of Mahatma Gandhi* (Clarendon Press, Oxford, 1987), III:544.

24. Gandhi, M. K. *The Story of My Experiments with Truth: An Autobiography* (Beacon Press, Boston, 1957), 202.

25. Tendulkar, D. G. *Mahatma* (Publication Division of the Government of India, New Delhi, 1961), IV:72.

26. Pyarelal. *Mahatma Gandhi: The Last Phase* (Ahmedabad, Navijivan, 1958), I:410.

27. Tagore, R. N. In Tendulkar, D. G. *Mahatma* (Publication Division of the Government of India, New Delhi, 1961).

28. Tendulkar, D. G. *Mahatma* (Publication Division of the Government of India, New Delhi, 1961), VIII: photo opposite 89.

29. Gandhi, M. K. "Necessity of Drawing Up a Balance Sheet," 1932. In Iyer, R. N., ed. *The Moral and Political Writings of Mahatma Gandhi* (Clarendon Press, Oxford, 1986), I:629.

# INDEX

on universality of humanity, 105;
voluntary poverty, 39-40;
vows of, 31-32, 141-42;
work in Champaran, 110-13
*Gandhi* (film), 3
General Electric, 106
General Motors, 22
Goals: establishing, 118-22;
measures of performance, 120
Golden Rule. *See* Universal code of
conduct

Habitat for Humanity, 75
*Hamlet*, 20
*Harijan*, 4, 35, 143
Higher standard of leadership.
*See* leadership
Hinduism, 4, 141
Hitler, Adolph, 2, 91

IBM, 22
Indian National Congress, 122,
130-31
*Indian Opinion*, 27-28
Inner Temple, the, 141
Integrity, 1;
in decision making, 109-16;
*vs.* infallibility, 7

Kasturbai, 141; death of, 143

L. L. Bean, 74
Leadership:
absolute values in decisions, 97-98;
by adults, 14;

and attachments, 38;
basic commitments, 17;
the challenge, 139;
commitment to openness, 46;
common characteristics, 39;
and double standards, 13;
evaluation, 28-29;
factors in, 1;
failure to see reality, 86;
Gandhi as example, 8;
identification with those led, 86;
personal service in, 78-79;
place of everyone, 139;
privileges of, 40-41;
and responsibility, 67;
responsibility for truth, 113;
self evaluation, 32;
and service, 59, 62;
service *vs.* power, 89-92;
setting examples, 63-64;
as trusteeship, 91-92;
and universal code of conduct,
63-64
Lexus, 74
Lincoln, Abraham, 39
Living truthfully, 20-22
London Theosophical Society, 141
London Vegetarian Society, 141
Lord Mountbatten, 78

MacArthur, Douglas, 2
Marshall, George, 39
Montgomery, Bernard, 2
Moral courage:
in business, 51-52;

# The Author

Dr. Keshavan Nair has over thirty years of experience in providing consulting services to corporations and government agencies in the United States and abroad. Prior to 1983 he was an Executive Vice President and a Director of Woodward-Clyde Consultants, a large, multidisciplinary, consulting firm. Since 1983 he has developed his own successful management consulting practice which focuses on leadership development and evaluation and improving the process and quality of strategic decision making. Dr. Nair was born in India and has a background in both Eastern and Western traditions, giving him the ability to examine leadership challenges from different philosophical and cultural traditions. His clients include small, emerging companies as well as Fortune 100 corporations.

He has been interviewed extensively on radio and television and for the print media regarding his views on leadership. He has also published widely in technical and management journals and is the author of *Beyond Winning, the Handbook for the Leadership Revolution.*

Dr. Keshavan Nair received his M.S. and Ph. D. in Engineering from Ohio State University, of which he has been elected a Distinguished Alumnus. He is also a graduate of the Advanced Management Program of the Harvard Business School. Dr. Nair maintains offices in Phoenix, Arizona and San Francisco, California.